THE

JOURNEY

STUDENT DISCIPLESHIP CURRICULUM

For Ages 12 – 22

Paul Sommer

THE

JOURNEY
STUDENT DISCIPLESHIP CURRICULUM

ISBN: 978-0-9981829-1-9

Printed in the United States of America

RevMedia Publishing
P.O. Box 5172
Kingwood, TX 77325
www.revmediapublishing.com

1 2 3 4 5 6 7 8 9 10 11   21 20 19 18 17 16 15 14

Table of Contents

Foreword

Paul's curriculum, "The Journey" is versatile and perfect for any size Bible study group, accountability group, or for personal growth. Personally, I was discipled by Paul myself and later used his curriculum to disciple others. I have enjoyed using it to study with close friends, for keeping one another accountable and diligently studying God's Word. The "Journey" follows the Scriptures closely and the questions bring the reader to a place of personal application. I have used this curriculum personally to teach and equip students in middle, high school and college. Each time, it brings insight and revelation to both the students and myself. Furthermore, it will also help students to learn to ask the right questions and know how to properly research when studying God's word.

This resource has brought blessings to me as well as many of the students and adults that have studied alongside me. I took advantage of this resource in high school and it helped me throughout college, and is still useful and relevant to me today as I continue into my career path. Words cannot express my gratitude and appreciation I have for Paul, his family, and for this valuable resource that God has used to bless many others and myself. I pray that others will choose to utilize this resource and grow deeper in their walk with the one true God of the universe.

Sincerely,

Kevin Vo

Follower of Christ, Brother and Friend

Houston, TX

Introduction

<u>It is very important that you read the entire introduction due to the fact that it will help you to understand the "why" and "how" of going through this curriculum/bible study.</u>

First I would like to personally welcome you to "The Journey," the discipleship curriculum/bible study that allows you to see your true history. You may read this and ask, "How do you know my history?" Scripture says that you have been adopted into God's family (Romans 8:12-16), so on the day that you received Jesus Christ as your Lord and Savior, you inherited a rich history that goes all the way back to Adam. This is why your study will begin at the beginning. When you read a book, you cannot totally understand it by starting in the middle or the end, so why would learning about God and your Godly heritage be any different? Understanding this family history will help you in your journey.

Secondly, I would like to explain briefly why you are even doing what is called "discipleship." When you become a believer, you are to become a disciple (in fact many verses in the Bible say that you are not part of the kingdom of God unless you are a disciple, or walking in covenant, so you are doing what is right in the eyes of the LORD). In 2 Timothy 2:1-2, Paul writes to a young pastor that he has been "discipling" or mentoring, and says, "You then, my child, be strengthened by the grace that is in Christ Jesus, and what you have heard from me in the presence of many witnesses entrust to faithful men who will be able to teach others also." Paul was discipling Timothy and now Timothy is to disciple men in his day until this day in which you are now studying this as part of your discipleship. *Take a moment this week to thank those that helped you to get this far and those that will be with you through this journey.* You see, salvation is a journey that began the day that God revealed Himself to you by His grace, you responded by repenting, putting your faith in Him and are now called to be obedient. From that day until your last breath, you will walk in the same cycle of grace, repentance, faith, and obedience. These terms will be defined throughout your studies over this next year.

This study is designed to take you one day at a time, growing as you go along this journey, one step at a time. Let me ask you a question, "Do you know more in school now than you knew a year ago (same question if you are not in school)?" I know that your answer is yes because we are always learning. Remember this fact as you are going through the curriculum. There will be days when you may not understand everything and things will be brand new, but that is okay. I do not expect you to know every word, which is why I define many words for you along the way. I also know that some of your schoolwork is tough as well, but in order to pass you must keep studying or get help. This is no different except you get the privilege of studying the words of God, the One who made you and loves you. Does that get you excited? The "Journey" is designed to help you along this path of discipleship, so be encouraged and know that at the end of one year, you will know more than when you started. Also, this curriculum is designed to teach you, but not to give you too much. Therefore, allow God to teach you each week and expect your knowledge and wisdom to grow. "For the LORD gives wisdom; from His mouth come knowledge and understanding"- Proverbs 2:6. The bible also says in James 1:5, "If any of you lacks wisdom, let him ask God, who gives generously to all without reproach, and it will be given him." So you can see from reading these scriptures, that if you want wisdom and knowledge, you must seek the One who gives these to those who ask sincerely. Paul says in 2 Corinthians 5:17- "Therefore if anyone is in Christ, he is a new creation. The old has passed away; behold the new has come. So now that you know this, are you ready to get started? Good, because I am so excited for you as you begin this "Journey." There are many different types of discipleship curriculum out there. I have designed this one "chronologically theological." It takes you through the whole Bible chronologically and defines theological terms along the way. My prayer is that it blesses you as much while you study it, as it has while I was writing it.

Okay it is time to start and I want to encourage you not to skip any portion of this introduction or any part of each lesson. This is not school and you don't get a grade, but you will gain much knowledge and wisdom from the time you spend in each lesson. **Some lessons can be done in 3-4 days, so if you finish quickly, don't just set it down and not look at it again for 2 weeks until your next lesson, but instead go back over it, ponder the questions, and you may come up with some questions of your own**. If you do, ask your parents or someone else you know that loves and walks with the LORD. When there is a question that seems more like you are giving your opinion because you don't know or are not sure what the answer is, put some thought into it. God asks that we worship Him in Spirit and in Truth (Read Hosea 4:6, Isaiah 5:13, John 4:23). If you still feel that you are unsure about the answer, pray and put some thought and research into it also. If you still feel that you are unsure about the answer, please contact me at *only1way.net*.

Remember, these lessons are not designed to give you more than you can handle, but instead are designed to help you build a foundation that you will equip you for the rest of your life. As a teacher of the Word of God, I have many books on my shelf that I think of as reference tools (books that I do not read straight through but refer to from time to time in order to get answers to certain questions). **This curriculum will be a study guide and a reference tool for you to refer back to for many years. Put it in a safe and convenient place in order to easily refer to it as the need arises.**

Before you begin the following four steps to each lesson, pray to God. Remember that prayer is learned- Luke 11:1 says, "Lord, teach us to pray." Look to our Master Yeshua (Jesus) to teach you how to pray. Go by his example and teachings in this area. Let us look at the four steps. <u>First,</u> you will have a section that will take you through some passages in which you will be asked to answer some questions and/or fill in some blanks. I encourage you to do each lesson in 3-4 days and then go back over it, but some of you study differently, so you may take only 3-4 questions each day. Either way, just do your best before your Creator who loves you.

<u>Second,</u> you will be encouraged to learn a memory verse. **Always look at the end of each lesson to get your memory verse, so you can start memorizing it as you are going through your lesson.** Do not wait until the end and then only memorize it for a day, but forget it the next day. Let God's Word become part of who you are. I have heard many people say they cannot memorize Scripture, but let me give you some suggestions that have worked for myself as well as many others. Yes, you can do it. You have a young mind. If I can do this at my age (I am older than many of your parents), you can do it as well.

There are 3 great ways to memorize Scripture:

1. Carry it around with you on a 3x5 card and read it over and over again until you can do it without looking

2. Take what it says and intentionally put it into practice.

3. Teach someone else like a friend or your parents. The accountability in teaching will help you learn it faster (this is my favorite way).

Third, you will be asked to read some additional passages that relate to this section and you will see these throughout your lessons. I encourage you to read out loud. Do this when you are alone or better yet, read to your family. Start with your baby brother or sister, if you have one. They may enjoy it and you will hear it as well as you read it. This gets one more sense involved in learning process. The idea is not how good you read or how fast you read, but that it gets in your head and heart.

Fourth, you will be asked to take a moment and journal. Yes this involves writing down your thoughts, your fears, your dreams, your prayers and any other thoughts you may have. (Yes, you guys can do this too. You are not too tough to do this, as tougher men have been doing this for centuries). God knows your thoughts anyway, but God is not forgetful like you are. Write them down so some day you can look back at them. Don't worry! No one is watching you except God, so just write or type away.

I would strongly encourage you to do the lessons on your own, but then meet in a small group, but if on your own, then meet with someone else to go over the answers, to think together about the questions that don't always have exact answers. This is what I did for several classes when I was going to seminary. It is a great way to have fellowship and strengthen one another in study and in prayer. Talk to your pastor or youth leader and begin to organize this as a weekly time to meet. If not, one to one is good as well.

You will also notice that I will continually talk about the Bible as the truth, as redemptive history or similar terms like these. I do this because of verses like 2 Peter 1:20-21, "Knowing this first of all that no prophecy of Scripture comes from someone's own interpretation. For no prophecy was ever produced by the will of man, but men spoke from God as they were carried along by the Holy Spirit." You can also refer to 2 Timothy 3:16-17, Hebrews 4:12, Psalm 19. Through my years of study, I have found that archaeologically, scientifically, and historically, the Bible is always proven right and never proven wrong. Thus I hold on to it and believe in it with all that I am each day. Remember that the Bible is true and from God. However, all the decisions of where to end sentences, paragraphs, paragraph headings, and many punctuations as well as chapters and verses were added later to make things easier to read. Therefore, errors in these areas are possible. Don't rely solely on the extra notes or commentary, but read what it actually says. Yes it is safe to read and trust your Bible to lead you to truth. Remember, you are accountable before God for your decisions, so let God speak to you as you study. You will also notice that I use very little reference material, other than my Hebrew and Greek reference materials. In other words, I will let Scripture interpret Scripture as much as I can. This way, you get more Scripture and less of my personal opinion. I realize that I am not perfect and thus I have humbly approached this project with much prayer. I pray that through this you will be led to grow in the LORD and desire Him more than anything else. Following God is not something you do only on certain days or in certain situations, but in all that you do (Colossians 3:17).

There is one last point and it is the most important point. If you complete all the lessons in this discipleship curriculum, but continue to live in sin and do not change, then you have missed the whole point. You do not become a disciple because you complete discipleship programs year after year, but you become a disciple when your life imitates the best disciple-maker and teacher of all time—Jesus the Christ (Yeshua the Messiah).

All quotes from the Bible will be from the ESV (English Standard Version) unless otherwise noted. If you do not have an ESV, you can go to www.bible.cc and access this version plus many other versions of the bible.

<u>Symbols and Words Used to Help You Study:</u>

- This will be the most common symbol or bullet point and it will be typical questions for you to answer. There will be fill in the blank, short answer, T or F, and circling the right answer.
- ➢ This will be your symbol for questions that you are to personally <u>think</u> about for your own life. Some will not necessarily have a simple wrong or right answer, but for you to <u>think</u> and <u>write</u> about. These are perfect <u>discussion</u> questions.
- ❖ Definitions of words and this list will also be at the end of the curriculum.
- ✓ This will be a list of items to help bring a concept together.
- ▪ Illustrations to help you better understand an idea or concept.
- ❖ **Extreme Thought or Critical Thought**- These terms are used for important topics and to help you think in a way that goes against the cultural (often against God) ways.
- ❖ **Definitive Thought or Idea**- These terms are used as I somewhat define a thought or idea, but leave some of it to you to think through.

Ask yourself the following questions as you are learning and journaling. Remember some of these questions will be easier for you now and others will become easier as you grown so no worries. Just use this as a guideline. On the first few lessons, I will walk you through this step by step and suggest some things to pray and think about. On later lessons, use the examples that have been put in place for you and you will pray and think on your own at the end of each day and each lesson.

1. Observation- What do I see?
2. Interpretation- What does it mean?
3. Correlation- How does it fit together?
4. Application- How do I put this into practice?
5. Illustration- How has the principle worked in other areas and in other people's lives?
6. Proclamation- How do I communicate this truth to others?
7. Motivation- How do I encourage others to love God by obeying God?

1. **Engage yourself in history, the biblical truths.**
2. **Six questions to ask while reading the text each time.**
   - Who?
   - What?
   - When?
   - Where?
   - Why?
   - How?
3. **Application**
   - How does this biblical truth affect how I live my life each day?

Okay, grab a red or blue pen so as to differentiate your answers from the questions, and begin your Journey.

© Paul Sommer   *www.only1way.net*

Lesson 1- Creator God

This first lesson covers Genesis chapters 1-2. I will keep most of the lessons to simply looking at the English, but there is something extremely important in the first verse of the Bible in the original Hebrew language. Created is *bara* in Hebrew and covenant is *berit* in Hebrew, both of which come from the same root word. In other words, God created you to be in covenant with Him. He did not just create mankind to simply wander about or live for himself so if someone asks you about your purpose in life, you can tell him or her "you were created to bring God glory." This means that everything you do, you do it in obedience to the covenant you are in with God. This will make more sense later, but for now it is important to understand how incredible it is that the only true God, the God of the universe knows you and loves you this much.

Please read each chapter completely before answering any questions. Remember what you read in the "Introduction" about following all directions. I know some weeks will be easier than others, but pray for God's help and honor him by your genuine efforts as you **worship Him through study**.

1. God created _____ things by His spoken _____. Genesis 1:1-3 (chapter 1, verses 1-3 just in case you did not understand what the numbers mean throughout your Bible).

2. God created all things in _____days and rested on the _____(Sabbath) day. Genesis 1:31-2:4. The bible says that God created the world in 6 days and we only have about 6000 years of recorded history, so how does this differ from what you are being taught in movies, media and museums, about Darwinian Evolution? Write some differences. If you do not know much about this subject, go to www.answersingenesis.org in order to understand what this is all about— Creationism vs. Darwinian Evolution. Write down something you learn about this subject you did not know before.

   • God created all things in 6 days, so would this include the dinosaurs?

3. "In the beginning _____. If you believe these 4 words, the rest of the Bible and life makes more sense. Any thoughts as to why this is so?

4. In Genesis 1:1, you read that God created the heavens and the earth. Now you get to read about how He did it each day. What did God create on each day?

- Day One

- Day Two

- Day Three

- Day Four

- Day Five

- Day Six

➤ On day 4, your Bible probably uses the word "seasons," and some of your Bible versions may have a footnote that says "appointed times." This is the correct translation as you will see further in these studies. This word in Hebrew focuses upon God creating times throughout the year that are Holy days set aside for Him, in order to meet with Him and specifically focus on exalting Him and putting all of your "important" things aside for your King. To further dwell upon this idea of what seasons really means, do you think that Adam and Eve went through weather of 110 degrees or -30 below in the garden?

- Anything interesting in the order of things considering what you know from science? Also look in Revelation 22 and what do you see that replaces the sun, moon and stars.

5. God created all things in 6 days and everything after that, which includes _____ (write in your full name). Genesis 1:27, 2:7, Psalm 139:13-16.

What happened on day 7? Write what you think, but you will learn more in later lessons. 3. God is not a man and thus does not need rest, then why do you think he did this? See Mark 2:27, John 4:24, Numbers 23:19, Leviticus 23:3, Hebrews 4:8-11.

- God created all things and said that it was all _____ good! Genesis 1:31
  - ➢ All created things were good, so do you think God created evil? (Isaiah 45:7 and check multiple translations. There is a difference between evil and God using His creation for judgment).

6. Man is made in the _____ of God as His highest creation. Genesis 1:26-27.
   - What was man's responsibility when it came to the other created beings? Genesis 1:26-30.

   - What was man's most important responsibility in chapter one? Be _____ and _____.

7. God places man in the garden or God's dwelling place with man (i.e. God's tabernacle or house). This was God's first house, or dwelling place, of intimacy with man.
   - God places Adam in the garden to do what? To _____ _____ and _____ _____. 2:15.   You could say that Adam's first occupation was as a _____. Actually to be serious, his first job was to protect and take care of God's house like a priest would. You will learn more about priests and God's dwelling place (house) later.

   - This is God's house so do you think there are any rules? What was your first thought or reaction when you saw the word "rules?" Is this a correct view of rules? Are there rules in your house? Are rules necessary to make the world function properly?

- What was the most important rule or commandment? Genesis 2:16-17

- Do God's instructions seem clear?

8. Adam's second _____ was being a taxonomist (naming the animals. 2:19). Seriously, this job was still secondary compared to being the priest.

9. Was man designed to be alone? 2:18

10. Man was formed from the _____ and woman was formed from _____. Genesis 2:7, 2:22.

11. In verse 24, you will see the first _____ and this union is designed by God.

   - Since this is God's design, can man just make his own rules about it and get divorced whenever he wants?

   - Man and woman shall become "one" flesh. This word one means more than just being one sexually or physically, but it means one spiritually, emotionally, physically and sexually. This is a bond that is never to be separated by man. (If you are not sure of this, you can look at relationships where a girl stays with an abusive guy, and many times tries to justify it. It is because of this "one" flesh truth, whether married or not). 1 Corinthians 6:15-20

12. So does sex as God designed it have any ugly or perverted meaning behind it as our culture always says? Genesis 1:28, 2:25

   - Sex is good when it is according to God's design for marriage between one

     _____ and one _____.   I Thessalonians 4:3-7, Hebrews 13:4, 1 Corinthians 6:14-20, Romans 1:26-27, Proverbs chapters 5-7.

     ➢ Is this teaching about sex different from much of what you see on TV and hear from your friends?

     ➢ Can sex outside of marriage or homosexuality be something that God approves of according to the above verses?

     ➢ How many ways can you think of that man has found to multiply outside of marriage?

- The LORD uses 3 words to give a similar command (be fruitful, multiply and fill the earth). He is basically talking about having children. There is a physical idea but with everything physical, God teaches you spiritually. Throughout much of scripture, you will see "bearing fruit" to mean walking in righteousness. God wants you to bear good fruit, just as He wanted Adam and Eve to bear good fruit. He wanted them to have children and then train them in obey His commands (walk in righteousness). Read Deuteronomy 6:4-9, Matthew 3:10, 7:17-19, Luke 6:43, John 15:1-8.

A. Memory Verse- Genesis 1:1-2. Additional verse- Genesis 2:16-17. <u>Write it down on a 3x5 card, put it on your phone, hang it on your mirror in your bedroom, on the refrigerator, etc. Learn it, live it! First thing to do is write it right here. You will right it out after each lesson.</u>

Remember to read all the verses that were mentioned throughout the lesson. This lesson is to be done over 2 weeks. <u>There are many ways in which you could do this, but the idea is not to wait until day 13, cram real fast like you do for a test for school and then wait another 13 days to do Lesson 2. This is not really the best way to learn what God wants to teach you. Here is a suggestion—spend 30-45 minutes per day until you finish and look at your memory verse each day. Then review before you begin the next lesson. See how this works.</u>

<u>Engage yourself in history, the biblical truths.</u>

➢ What do you think it would have been like to be Adam, the first man who was able to walk and talk with Creator God in a world without sin, without struggles?

➢ Since a caring, loving and perfect God created you, how does this help you when you look at your life each day? How does this compare with believing Darwinian Evolution (macroevolution), where you came into existence by chance, evolving from monkeys?

B. Six questions to ask while reading the text each time.

1. Who created you? What does this mean in your daily decisions?

2. What is this section of biblical truth about (part of answer is found in 1:14) and what is your purpose if created by a Holy and Perfect God?

3. When did this take place?

4. Where did these events take place? Are there any clues or any names of places?

5. Why do you think God made so many different things?

6. How does the fact that God created you and loves you, (not created by chance) change your view of life and your purpose?

C. Application How does this biblical truth affect how I live my life each day? Will this change how you look at other people in light of Genesis 1:26-27?

D. Journal and prayer time. Is there a sin you need to confess? As you do this, ask God to help you live out what you just studied?

Lesson 2 - Gracious God

Read Genesis chapter 3 completely before starting. Remember where you left off on the last lesson. Genesis 2:25 says, "And the man and his wife were both naked and were not ashamed." There was no sin and thus no shame. Remember to look at the memory verse at the end of each lesson so you can memorize it and know it very well by the time you finish the lesson.

1. God created all things and said that it was _____ _____ Genesis 1:31.

2. What and who does the serpent represent in 3:1(Isaiah 14:12-15. (Hint: There are rules in God's house).

3. The serpent questions the authority and character of _____?

4. In Genesis 2:9, how many trees are mentioned in the Garden?
   - Does it say that God placed the tree of the knowledge of good and evil in the Garden? Was the tree itself bad?

   ➤ Who planted it? Could the serpent have planted it there or did God do it out of His goodness or some explanation in between? What tree do you read about when Jesus the Messiah returns at the end? Matthew 15:13, Revelation 22:2

   ❖ **Definitive Idea (Mixing)**- What type of life will you live if you mix good and evil? God hates when you mix what is good with what is evil. This is an important truth throughout scripture. A great example is found here and in Acts 5:1-10. Are you doing this right now and if so, how?

5. Compare God's command in Genesis 2:15-18 with what the woman says in chapter 3:3. How important is it to carefully listen to what God actually says without adding or taking away from His words?

6. The serpent questions God's words again in 3:4-5 and says that by eating of it they will gain knowledge of both _____ and _____.
   - Do you think they already knew what was good? _____ They knew good by knowing who? _____. What benefit would it bring to them to know evil? Can you think of some things that you have seen on TV, the Internet, or have experienced that were

sinful (evil) and you wish now you did not know? Romans 6:20-21. Another important issue is that in knowing good and evil, they wanted to be God. Do we still see this desire in our current culture and can you name any?

- What was God extending toward them by commanding them not to eat of the tree of the knowledge of good and evil? Psalm 119:64, 4:8, 36:7.

  ➤ As you study God's tabernacle (temple) later, God has rules in his "house" and this is part of God's rules or loving boundaries for his people. Do you need love and safety (boundaries) in your life or do you think you should do whatever you want because you already know everything? Take a moment and think of something that you have done where you thought you knew everything and later realized that you should have listened to someone wiser than you.

7. What were the first sins (these 2 go together) of man that occurred in 3:6? _____ and _____. See Proverbs 16:18, Romans 5:19, 1 John 2:16

   - Why is sin (unrighteousness) a problem? Psalm 116:5, Daniel 9:14, Romans 2:13, 3:23, Galatians 3:11.

   ❖ **Sin Defined** (Chattah in Hebrew)- This is an archery term that means "a missing of the target." [1] The target is obedience to God and His perfect laws (teachings) and when we disobey, we miss that perfect mark. God's measure of morality is the original mark that all actions must be measured against. Our sin puts us in a place of dishonor and shame, which takes away from the glory of God that is in us. When we sin, we are not living to bring God glory, but are living in a manner that dishonors God. By sinning, we are exchanging the glory of the Immortal God for our own glory. We must seek to live in a way that restores honor and thus brings honor and glory to our King and Creator. (Also see Romans 3:23, Joshua 7:11, Psalm 66:2, 1 Samuel 15:24, Matthew 5:16, and 1 John 3:4).

8. What are the two types of people in the world (there are only 2)? Which one does God give His favor? 1 Peter 3:18, 1 Corinthians 6:9, Luke 1:6, Psalm 32:11

> ➤ Does sin ever just affect you? Think about what you just read.

- What did the woman do after she ate? 3:6

- What happened in verse 7 and compare it to Genesis 2:25?

9. What were the consequences of the first sins? Genesis 3:7-11, Psalm 25:3, Luke 9:26, Romans 6:21.

10. What was the 3rd sin in verses 12-13? _____(denial of _____)
See 2 Samuel 22:24, Psalm 18:23, 5:10, 25:11, Isaiah 6:7, Genesis 6:9.

11. Who was cursed after sin entered the world (3:14)?

- In verse 15, God says that there will be hostility or enmity between your seed and the seed of the woman. For now, the word "seed" means children, offspring or descendants, but it can also refer to the Messiah and the Word of God.

- What do these 2 seeds represent? The seed of the _____ and the seed of the

   _____ . Refer back to 6b. Also read Romans 16:20, Ephesians 1:22-23,

   Revelation 12:17.

   > ➤ The next time you look at the world and its struggles or you notice that almost every movie is about good (righteous) and evil (unrighteous), now you know where that comes from. As you look at the news of the Middle East, know that this battle of the seeds has been going on for a long time. Satan vs. God and His redeemed. Satan will lose but he will be hostile as long as he can. John 10:10.

12. The man and woman were not cursed, but what did their sin bring?

- What were the 2 consequences for the woman's sin mentioned in verse 16?

   > ➤ Did you ever wonder what childbirth would be like if there were no sin?
   > ➤ Did you ever wonder why marriage can be so difficult?

13. What were the 3 consequences for the man's sin mentioned in verses 17-19?

- Man was supposed to lead his home, to be the leader (priest) of his home.
- Where does your food come from? Someone has to deal with the thorns and thistles so you can eat.
- Do you ever mow your yard? Do you see weeds? Do you sweat? Now you know where this began.
- Men have to work but they would have done it without sweating and toiling.
- It is tempting to be prideful and blame the first man and woman, but remember this is two of the first sins committed. The fruit does not fall far from the original tree.

14. Who does God hold responsible for the first sin? Romans 5:12, Ephesians 5:25-26.

15. Is work part of the consequences or did God command work before the fall of man? Gen. 2:15

16. What characteristic of God enters the picture in history at this point? Read all of these- Genesis 2:17, 3:20, 6:8, Romans 5:15.

- Did God lie or did he extend grace? He said "you will surely die" and then the first woman is named Eve, which means mother of all living. Did they however die? Without God's grace you would not be here today. It would have been perfectly just and right for God to wipe them out but He did not do it this way. Awesome!!

- ❖ **Grace defined-** (Chen, pronounced Cane in Hebrew)- To give or show favor or beauty. What a beautiful picture, as God does not end mankind, but extends favor to allow mankind to continue their seed or offspring. Man deserved death and God let him continue life. [2] There is more than one word for grace in Hebrew, but the idea is of unmerited favor. Nothing you can do on your own on either side of salvation is accomplished without grace. However, grace is also tied to a covenant with God. In other words, you cannot save yourself, but you are responsible within the covenant to work out your salvation with fear and trembling (obedience) with the help of God as we see in Philippians 2:12 and 1 Corinthians 15:1-2, Galatians 2:21.

17. How did man attempt to deal with sin in 3:7 and how did God deal with their sins in 3:21?

- The phrase "clothed them" means to cover or atone in Hebrew. God covered your sin so that He could have a relationship with you. God (righteous) cannot dwell with man (sinful or unrighteous). When you enter into salvation, you enter into a blood (blood represents life) covenant. You will learn more about this when you learn about Abram (Abraham). God could have killed you, shed your blood and been right to do so, but he allowed the animal to shed his blood and symbolically take your place.

- God extends grace, but there are still consequences for sin. Man cannot live forever as sinful creatures, so man must leave God's house. God's act of having them leave was extending grace and justice. Many convey a message of intolerance or hatred about God from this, but it was actually the opposite.

  ➢ As you end chapter 3 of Genesis, you may be asking why couldn't God just forgive them totally and not make them leave. The Bible is written as a legal document so God will never break His own laws of the universe except for the betterment of mankind. In other words, you will see later how God alters the laws of His creation in His grace, but that does not mean God broke a law. When man sinned, he broke covenant (legal document), the laws of God and thus brought condemnation and consequences upon himself. You will learn more about covenant later. God did not condemn but instead His perfect moral law is in place and man broke it. God is consistent with His character and nature, meaning that God will always do God things. He will always be loving, righteous, just, kind and so forth. And in all of these, He will be holy or set apart as different. Your sin deserved death, but God extended grace, love and justice (he loved mankind enough to allow them to avoid living forever in their sin), which extended life. But life is now full of sin, so it is tougher and contains death (God did still keep His original word but the death was not instant), but each man or woman can make a choice to follow Him when He reveals this truth. Through this choice, you can have eternal life, not just the temporary earthly life. Take a moment and thank him for this salvation that is available. John 3:16-20.

A. **Memory Verse**- Genesis 3:20-21 (write it out).

B. Six questions to ask while thinking back through the text.

1. Who were the characters of Genesis 3?

2. What should Adam have done when Eve offered him the fruit?

3. When should Eve have quit listening to the serpent?

4. Where was Adam as he was head of the family?

5. Why did Adam and Eve know they were naked?

6. How did God take care of their sins?

C. Application How does this biblical truth affect how I live my life each day? Does this explain what you see in the news each day or what you see in your family and friends?

D. Journal and prayer time. Is there a sin you need to confess? As you do this, ask God to help you live according to what you have just studied. Praise God for His amazing grace from the beginning.

Lesson 3: Righteous God

As you see different titles for each lesson, please do not think this is the only thing we are seeing about God, but it is just a way to introduce another characteristic of God and different lessons you can learn. God is always all of these chapter titles and so much more. Read Genesis chapters 4:1-8:19. Yes I know that this is a lot, but when it comes to the foundational chapters of the bible, I don't want you to skip anything. There are people that have dedicated their lives to trying to convince you that Genesis chapters 1-11 are just a myth and some go as far as to teach that all of Genesis is a myth. You need to know the truth about God as it unfolds. Keep reading.

The setting is changed from God's house (dwelling place) to God's world. In other words, God is in ultimate control, but Satan (represented by the serpent) is now allowed temporary control. Ephesians 2:1-2. So in God's world, it is still about righteous and unrighteous or good and evil choices. With this in mind, let us begin Genesis chapter 4.

1. Adam and Eve have two sons and their names are _____ and _____.

2. Cain and Abel are asked to bring offerings before the LORD.

   - **Offering defined**- In Hebrew this word literally means rest. It also means "what is brought to another." [3] You are sinful in nature but you want to be near God. Remember God cannot dwell with sinful man. Thus you must come with an offering brought by a righteous and humble heart so that you can be near God and find rest.

   - Abel brings the _____ of his flock. 4:4

   - Cain brings an _____ of the fruit of the ground. 4:3

   - Some say that Cain and Abel had to figure out how to please God, because there were no laws from God yet. Would a loving and just God confuse them like this or do you see some instructions already in previous chapters?

   - What was the difference between the two offerings?

   - Why did God accept Abel's and reject Cain's?

3. What did Cain do to Abel after God did not accept his offering?

   - What were Cain's sins and when did they begin? Genesis 4:3, 4:7-8, Matthew 5:21.

- Did Cain have a choice? Ephesians 4:26, James 1:13-15.

- Even though Cain sinned and was cursed, God extended grace and

  _____ to him. Joshua 20:1-3

3. Do you like music? What was the first musician's name and what instruments did he play? 4:21. You thought the first musicians were Elvis or the Beatles. LOL.

4. Adam and Eve have another son and his name is Seth.
   - Seth's first grandchild is named Mahalel, meaning "praise of God." As you will learn later, the blessing and birthright were supposed to go to the firstborn, but this is not what happens with Cain, but instead it goes through the righteous son Abel, who is substituted or appointed by Seth and so forth from there.

5. Is there anything that can be learned from a lineage? It seems boring to read all these names and how many years people lived. Most of us do not study our own lineage. I pray after reading my next comments you will change your mind and realize that as you grow as a disciple, every word from God is important and can teach you something.

6. Genealogy

   - Adam – Man
   - Seth – Appointed
   - Enosh – Mortal
   - Kenan – Sorrow
   - Mahalalel – The blessed God
   - Jared – Shall come down
   - Enoch – Teaching
   - Methuselah – His death shall bring
   - Lamech – The Despairing
   - Noah – Comfort and rest

     - So what does this say? _Man appointed mortal sorrow. The blessed God shall come down teaching. His death shall bring the despairing comfort and rest_. Wow! This is not about Bible codes, but about an amazing God. Understand that you serve a big God that is into the details of His Word and of your life.

7. The state of man at the time of Noah was only _____ continually? Genesis 6:5

8. But Noah found _____ in the eyes of the LORD. 6:8

   - Why did Noah find favor (grace) in the eyes of the LORD? 6:9

   - The earth is filled with _____ so God is going to destroy man with His creation. 6:13

9. What does God tell Noah to build? 6:14

   - Why will this be necessary? 6:17

   - Can Noah build it his way or are there specific instructions? 6:14-16

10. God establishes a _____ with Noah. Genesis 6:18.

11. Covenant is a word you are probably not familiar with, but for now just know that when God does this, He cannot break it or He would be a liar. Numbers 23:19, Titus 1:2, Hebrews 6:18.

12. Noah receives instructions about filling the ark. He is to get animals after their own kind, which means that you need two dogs, two cats, etc., one _____ and one _____. 6:19.

    - More specifically, what does God say about gathering animals in 7:1-3?

    - In 6:21, Noah is supposed to gather every sort of _____.

13. Notice that Noah did _____ that God had _____ him.

    ➢ How do you think obeying all instead of part of what God says will affect your daily walk with Him? Remember what you have learned about Him so far.

14. How many people were saved on the ark? Can you name them?

15. Who shut the door to the ark? How tough would it have been for Noah to do this and why?

➤ Would you be able to stand respectfully against your family if you knew they were leading you away from God?

16. The waters were above the mountains over 22 feet (15 cubits).
   ➤ If the water was high enough to cover the mountains, could this have been a local flood or would it have been a worldwide flood? You are taught in school according to Darwinian evolution, that the flood is a myth or that it was a local flood? Look at Genesis 9:11 and if it was a local flood, then God is a _____, because there are floods around the world each year.

17. How long did it take Noah to build the ark? Do a little research.

   • With the above information, could you say that God extended _____ to everyone before He shut the door?
   • God is _____! Genesis 18:25, Psalm 111:7, Philippians 4:8.

18. What command does God give in 8:17? Has God changed His command from Genesis 1:28?

   ➤ Some of you may be having a difficult time when you think about the story of the flood and the fact that so many animals and people died. How can God be **just**? Remember that Noah is building an ark in a land where there was no water nearby and it had never rained. So building an ark would have drawn a lot of attention. All the people of the earth lived in the same area at that time and they all had a chance to repent of their sins and turn to God, but they chose not to. God is in control but man still has freewill to make choices. Just as people will choose today to reject God and die, **earning** them eternity separated from God, people did the same in the days of Noah. Read Genesis 6:1-5 and John 3:16-20.

   A. Memory Verse- Genesis 6:9. Additional verses- Gen. 6:5

B. Six questions to ask while thinking back through the text.

1. Who was saved and who was not?

2. What happened to those that rejected God?

3. When did Noah know that there was no turning back for anyone else?

4. Where did Noah find safety?

5. Why did God bring judgment?

6. How did Noah respond when asked to build the ark?

C. Application- How does this biblical truth affect how I live my life each day? Does this explain what you see in the news each day or what you see in your family and friends?

D. Journal and prayer time. Is there a sin you need to confess? As you do this, ask God to help you live according to what you have just studied. What can you praise God for today?

Lesson 4: Just God

Congratulations! You have now completed 3 lessons along this discipleship journey. Take a moment and pat yourself on the back, give yourself a high five, or crank up your favorite song; i.e. whatever you want to do to be encouraged up to this point. Another important tip is if you run across a word you do not know, Google it on a couple of websites and get a definition; at least one of the websites should be biblically-based website or wikipedia (avoid urbandictionary.com). Many words that I now use I had to look up at some point. Don't just skip it and say it does not matter. Take the high road and gain knowledge with a little more work. Next, I want you to take notice that in the last 3 lessons, there are several extra verses within the lesson. Since you have two weeks to do each lesson, take the time to read all of those verses out loud if possible as you go through the lesson or read some during the lesson and others later.

You may be asking "why out loud?" You do not have to read out loud, but the more of your 5 senses you get involved in your learning process, the more you will remember and I pray the more you will apply to your life. Many of these other verses will be needed in order to get the correct answers. There is power in the Word of God, so don't take away any chance you get to read it. The average Christian only reads the Word of God less than 30 minutes per week. This is what the polls have said for many years now. I challenge you to desire a deeper walk with God than just the average. The fact that you are doing these lessons complete in their entirety puts you above average and you are not just reading, but studying so that it will really change your life. Read Genesis 8:20- chapter 11 before beginning.

1. Noah and his family just got off the ark with all the animals. What is the first thing Noah does when he gets off the ark? 8:20 Have you seen this pattern before? 4:3-5 8:20

- Where do we see this from before? 4:3-5

  ➢ When it says that the LORD was pleased by the smell of the offering, was that because God was hungry and Noah knew how to make that sacrifice smell like a great BBQ cookout?

- God was pleased with the _____of Noah. How does this compare with the state of man in 6:5?

- What does 8:22 tell us about what the flood did to God's creation?

> When you look at things like the Grand Canyon, when you hear about fossils of fish at the top of the tallest mountains, trees fossilized straight up in the side of a mountain, as well as other "unexplained" things in nature, remember that the flood is the only event that explains why things look the way they are and why there are so many fossils that occurred at the same time in history and in the condition to become fossils; see Cambrian Explosion at answersingenesis.org. I am including comments like this so that you will begin to think with a biblical worldview, to know that the Bible is absolutely true in every word, and is not in contrast with true science. You will begin to see and understand that God created all things, is in ultimate control of all things and is the designer of all things that make this world exist and function. He is not only Creator God, but has chosen to reveal Himself to you through His written Word, so keep studying to develop a biblical worldview (all answers for life come from the Bible).

2. What changed in Genesis 9:3? Compare to 1:28-29.

3. Why are you not to eat flesh with blood in it? Genesis 9:4

> What word lets you know that this command is still for us today? Genesis 9:4

4. Is it wrong to murder someone? 9:6, 1:27

❖ **Image defined**- This word is *tselem* in Hebrew and means shadow. [4] If you see me, you see God in me because I am a shadow of God. I am not exactly like God but the fingerprints of a holy God are upon me as His created being. So how does this help you when you look at issues like the following? Do a little research and write some thoughts about these crucial cultural subjects. Go to my website only1way.net and I did a 2-part series with great details on the issue of abortion.

✓ *Abortion and infanticide*- Is there ever a time when abortion is right according to these verses? Can our choice be more important than obedience to the One who gave life?

✓ *Euthanasia*- Is it right to help someone die when they are old or in pain?

✓ *Eugenics*- Look up Margaret Sanger (Planned Parenthood) and Adolph Hitler for some history on this subject. "Google" can be a wonderful thing.

5. Who was the covenant between in Genesis 9:9-10

- What was the sign of the covenant in 9:14?

  ➢ And you just thought they were nice to look at; now you know the history. Another cool fact about this sign is that the middle color is green. Have you ever wondered why? The trees, the grass and plants are mostly green and that is the color that can absorb all the colors of the sun so as to get the most nutrients. Our God thought of everything. The next time you think that God does not care about your life, remember how much he cares about the trees and plants. He cares even more about you. Matthew 6:30-34

6. From the sons of Noah, the whole world was to be dispersed, which means that somewhere in your lineage, you are kin to one of these three sons and their names were _____, _____, and _____.

7. How long did Noah live (9:29)? Did he know Adam? And you thought your parents were old?

8. In chapter eleven you will read about the story of the Tower of Babel, and what happened in 11:4? See 9:19 to see what they were supposed to do.

- So were they being obedient to God?

- Since they had decided to do what they wanted, God came down and confused their _____. 11:7

  ➢ Now you know where this began as well. **Have you figured out yet that anything you can think of somehow originated with God, for without God nothing would exist?** Look for more as you continue to read the Bible.

  - What does this tell us about God's character? He has _____over all things or He is sovereign. Acts 4:24, 1 Timothy 6:15.
  - So they discontinued building the Tower of _____ (means confusion or to mix).

A.   Memory Verse- Genesis 9:16

37

B. Six questions to ask while thinking back through the text.

1. Who initiated the covenant?

2. What was the first thing Noah did when he got off the ark?

3. When did Noah know that God would not do this again?

4. Where do all people come from according to chapter 10?

5. Why did God make a covenant?

6. How did the people begin to live again in chapter 11?

C. Application How does this biblical truth affect how I live my life each day? Is it important to be obedient to God, the God who creates and can destroy life if he chooses? Can I live a life without God in it daily?

D. Journal and prayer time. Is there a sin you need to confess and a praise to give God? What can you praise God for today. What is your heart thankful for today?

Lesson 5- Covenant God

Okay you have 12 chapters to read before beginning. Read Genesis chapters 12-23. Don't worry! It reads like a narrative (story) with different events associated with the main characters, so just think of it as a movie with a great plot but without the video screen. Remember as I said in the introduction about reading—it is not about how good or fast that you read, but that you read it. Read it to your parents, grandparents, aunts or uncles. I know they will be excited to hear you read the bible. They will learn too. If for some reason you really struggle to read, then get an app that will read the bible to you. Just open your bible and follow along as the narrator reads it.

Okay, do not forget that as you read the bible, these are not just "stories" or what some people call fables. Fables are not real. Stories, or God's history, involve real time, real people in a real world in real history! Is that enough "real" for you? Good because God is real, God is truth and this book you are reading is truth. This is a really good lesson. Really!

1. You read that all nations came from the 3 sons of Noah, so which son did Abram come from and what was his father's name? Genesis 11:10-27.

2. The bible now introduces, Abram, the first missionary, as some like to call him. God asks Abram to leave his land and his home and Abram obeys. This is what missionaries have been doing for centuries. Some of you may be called to be missionaries one day in order to be a light (shining in a dark world) so others may come to be disciples of God through Jesus Christ.

3. The LORD makes a 5-fold covenant with Abram
   ✓ I will make you a great nation.
   ✓ I will bless you.
   ✓ I will make your name great.
   ✓ I will bless those who bless you.
   ✓ I will curse those that curse you.

4. What else did God reveal in this statement to Abram in 12:3? See Galatians 3:7-8.
   • In Galatians 3:7-8, it says that God _____the gospel beforehand to Abraham.
   ❖ **Gospel defined** (Greek is *euangellion* from basar in Hebrew). It means "good news" to be celebrated and more specifically in biblical terms, the good news that God keeps his covenant with sinful man and brings salvation to man by grace through faith. [5] However, to participate in this good news, you must repent and live in repentance because if you do not do so, you cannot have a relationship with God. Even if you are saved and live, at times, in un-repentance, you are not in fellowship with God, thus not walking as a disciple in His favor. You are living for yourself. For those that do not come with a repentant heart, but a prideful heart, will choose to live without God and thus spend eternity in Hell, separated from God. (John 3:16-20, Ephesians 2;1-10). This good news

of salvation was revealed even more when it became physical reality in a man. Thus, the Word became flesh and "tabernacled" or dwelled on the earth and we know Him as Jesus the Messiah. Also see Isaiah 1:27, John 1:1, Genesis 1:3, James 4:4, Acts 2:37-40.

> ➤ **Did you hear a true gospel message?** Do you know that you are saved as a disciple of the Messiah, Jesus? If this is not what you heard and thought that you could live however you wanted, or are just "led by the spirit" (as some teach) as if the Spirit of God would lead you away from the laws of God, please pray to God and keep studying so you will know this cannot be true. If you find out that you misunderstood or were led to believe something else, get right with God by repenting (turning from sin and turning to righteousness), receive his grace and walk in faith and obedience. Now you can know you are saved and this is the way to live as a disciple everyday.

5. What land did God tell Abram to go to in Genesis 12:1-5?

- What was Abram's response when asked to leave his own country for a God that he didn't know real well yet? 12:1-4

- What part of the covenant does God state again in Genesis 12:7?

6. What did Abram do next in verses 7 and 8?

- Whenever you see this action in Scripture, (when done correctly and with a sincere heart) represents _____ (by offering a sacrifice).

  - ❖ **Worship defined** (*Shachah* in Hebrew)- "to pay respect or reverence to another by bowing low or getting on knees with face to the ground." [6] You are acknowledging that God is above you, He is to be feared and you owe Him everything including yourself. It is dying to self and acknowledging God for all of who He is, what He has done and bowing before Him in reverence and fear. Romans 14:11-12, Psalm 29:2, 96:9, Isaiah 66:23.

7. What does God show Abram as an illustration of His great promise? Genesis 15:5

- Abram responds in _____ and it is counted to him as _____.
  Genesis 15:6.

- Abram is saved by _____ and _____. Genesis 3:21 (Lesson 2 #14) and Genesis 15:6.

- What type of faith is a saving faith and was this Abram's faith? Genesis 12:4

- What two types of faith are there? There is a faith with _____ and a faith _____ works. James 2:14-26. In other words, if you say you have faith, but do nothing, your lack of action and obedience to God reveals you have no faith.

  ❖ **Faith (belief) defined**- (*Aman* or Emunah in Hebrew)- "To support, to trust or continuance. It is from a picture of a pillar that grabs hold or supports something else. To stand firm as a support. Also the passing (continuance) of strength or skill to the next generation." In Hebrews 11:1, the Greek word *hupostasis* means "that which stands under." [7]See, faith is not about sight, but about what you cannot see. It is not about observing, but about doing (action or obedience). It is not about our ability but the ability of Him who stands under you as you walk through this journey of life; the God of the universe. Will you trust God for who He is and continue this trust by passing it on to the next generation. It begins with your own family first.

  ▪ **Illustration of faith without works**—If you say you believe or have faith that if you lift weights, you will be stronger and in better health, but you never lift a single weight, then you have shown your faith is without works (no action or obedience).

  ➢ So how are you saved? By _____ through _____ unto good _____ (give a message of God through your actions). Ephesians 2:8-10. Remember in the introduction when I said that things like the verses were not inspired by God, but added by man. Here is a good example because verses 8-10 could easily be one verse defining salvation.

8. So how are you saved? By _____ through _____ unto good _____; (give a message of God through your actions). Ephesians 2:8-10- Remember in the introduction when I said that things like the verse numbers were not inspired by God, but added by man. Here is a good example because verses 8-10 could easily be one verse defining salvation. Are you saved by good works (your own ability), or are you to do good works after you are saved to reveal your salvation?

  ❖ **Salvation defined** (y'shua or yeshua in Hebrew)- This is one of the most important definitions to get right because everything else rests upon this in your life. It means "to be rescued or preserved out of trouble and into restoration with God." [8] Salvation is defined by me this way (combining Bible verses): "Salvation is by grace through a living, penitent and persevering faith in God through the living Messiah, Yeshua." Look back to gospel defined as well.

- ✓ *Grace* is unmerited favor; a free gift. Without grace we cannot be saved, but we have the option to reject God's grace and choose death over life. God is life.
- ✓ *Living*- you are alive and will live for eternity. You now have things to do. Ephesians 2:10. You are not defeated and under the control of Satan. Ephesians 2:1-2.
- ✓ *Penitent*-(Repentant)- You repent regularly before the LORD for your sins. This means that you make things totally right before your God and those whom you hurt. Numbers 5: 1-5,   2 Corinthians 7:9-11
- ✓ *Persevering*- You live this for as long as you live. You will have times of struggle in your life, but in general, you are bearing fruit (living in righteousness) for the LORD. 2 Timothy 4:7
- ✓ *Faith* is more about "who" than what. It is the object or focus of your faith that carries you through. Faith in you or other people will fail but faith in God will stand firm. Hebrews 11:1
- ✓ *Living Savior or Messiah*- God is alive and His Son is alive. Jesus is God's Son, who came and died, but he did not stay in the grave, but was resurrected on the third day, conquering death so that one day you can do the same. 1 Corinthians 15:3-4

- ➤ When you look at this definition of salvation, I pray that you take a look at your life and ask yourself some tough questions about how your life looks. I also want to remind you that this is God's truth of salvation, but this does not mean that everything will be easy. Do not get down on yourself. This leads to another point that is very important. A person that is saved is saved as an individual person, but salvation is not a selfish or individualistic thing. You are saved into a group (body) of believers, so you are not to do this alone, you are not to think you are alone, and you are not to think that your celebrations of obedience and your failures of disobedience should only affect and involve you. Start now in realizing that you need other people. Community is God's design for unity.

9. Who does God make the covenant with by the physical action in 15:12-17?

- • Who gets to be part of the blessings of the covenant? 15:18

- • What was Abram doing while God is passing through the dead animals?

- • How did Abram feel as He caught a glimpse of God's glory? 15:12

- • Why did God make the covenant with Himself? Read all- Exodus 32:13, Numbers 23:19, Isaiah 48:13, Malachi 3:6, Romans 3:23, Jeremiah 17:9.

- Did Abram participate in ensuring that this covenant would be upheld?

10. How was the "I will make you a great nation" statement playing out in Abram's mind? 13:16, 15:3-4, 16:1-2.

- Did Abram trust God or was he trying to help fulfill this for God? Genesis 16:1-6

10. What was the sign of the covenant between God and Abraham? 17:1-5

- Why do you think God would ask him to do this? Is it a spiritual or physical matter or both?

- How old was Abraham and Sarah when Isaac, the child of the promise, was born? What does this tell us about God and his promises? Luke 1:31-33, 37-38.

11. What does God ask Abraham to do in Genesis 22:1-2?

- How does Abraham respond in 22:1-2?

- What characteristic did Abraham display as he did in Genesis 15:6?

  ➢ Do you think he understood God's covenant with him?

- How far was the journey from Beersheba to Mt. Moriah? (There are no cars, trains or airplanes); use a map.

  ➢ Can you imagine some things that may have gone through his mind on a 3-day journey, knowing what God just asked him to do? What would you think about?

12. In Genesis 22:14, what do you think the phrase "as it is said to this day" means? John 8:56-58.

- Do you think all generations were awaiting Jesus the Christ since sin came into the world? (Jesus is Yeshua in Hebrew and Christ means ("anointed one" or Messiah).

- Also, God chose to reveal one of His names in this verse (Genesis 22:17). God will provide or God sees. How does this help you as you walk with him each day? Does this give you comfort as you follow him each day?

- What does God do in Genesis 22:17-18? Refer back to 15:5.

A. **Memory Verse-** Genesis 17:19

B. Six questions to ask while thinking back through the text.

   1. Who is the main character?

   2. What made Abram different?

   3. When did God test Abram's faith?

   4. Where does this take place?

   5. Why did God make a covenant with Himself?

   6. How did Abram respond to the presence of God?

C. Application- How does this biblical truth affect how I live my life each day?

D. Journal and prayer time. Is there a sin you need to confess? As you do this, ask God to help you live according to truth. Praise Him for His faithfulness.

Lesson 6- Isaac, Jacob and Esau (Family Matters)

Do you think Abraham is an awesome man? I pray that you want to walk in that kind of faith! Okay, you have learned a little about covenants and God's promises through them, so now it is time to move to the next generation that draws you closer to revealing the Messiah. See, each generation lived like they would see the Messiah return. They were not completely sure what that would look like but they had faith that it would happen. Jesus the Messiah will come again so keep studying His Word to know more about His first and second return. Read Genesis chapters 24-36 before beginning. Remember to look at your memory verse also.

- Does Abraham leave his son's marriage to chance? Why not? Genesis 15:4

- How did Abraham know what to do? You can look at Deuteronomy 6:4-9 and know the answer, but Abram did not have a Bible sitting in front of him. Even though the commandments of God had not been written down yet, God taught His children orally or through dreams and visions. He did this so they would know how they were to live, just like He did with Adam in the Garden. The LORD will always let us know what He expects.

1. Look at how God rewards Abraham's faithfulness in choosing properly for Isaac.
   - Abram puts someone he trusts to act for him to guide Isaac to make a wise decision. 24:1-9

   - Why could Isaac not marry a Canaanite? Genesis 9:22-26   Ham is the father of Canaan (Canaanites), who is cursed. Even though we do not know much about Abram's family, Abram trusts that a wife from his family will be better than from the cursed descendants of Canaan.

   - Abraham's servant stops to _____ in verse 12.
     - ➢ How long does it take for God to answer and will God always answer prayer that fast? 24:15, 45. Psalm 22:1-2. God will always answer prayers by yes, no or wait. God will answer prayer quickly but many times in life He does not answer immediately in order to teach you some things that you need to learn. God will not answer your prayers if there is intentional sin in your life. You cannot approach God in sin unless you come with a humble and repentant heart.

- List the characteristics of Rebekah. 24:15-21

- Was Isaac to marry Rebekah based on looks or was it based on something more than that? What was it?

- ➤ What else do you see about her in these verses that you would like in your future spouse? (if you are not married). Come on, you know you are checking him/her out, but what problem might this way of finding a spouse bring? It is okay to like how someone looks of course, but beauty fades and muscles sag, so you better look for something deeper than just that!

3. What did the servant do after he found Isaac's future spouse? 24:26

4. Laban was Abraham's great-nephew and Rebekah's _____. 24:29.

5. When did Isaac love Rebekah? 24:67

- ➤ What does this say about our current culture and the fact that "falling in love" and "falling out of love" are common terms? Is a marriage based on an emotional idea of love or is love based upon more than emotions? Can you trust your emotions or feelings? Jeremiah 17:9, Proverbs 14:12.

6. Abraham took another wife after Sarah died named <u>Keturah</u> and he lived for _____ years. 25:1-7.

7. Isaac and Rebekah have twins named _____ and _____. 25:23-26

- Esau was a man of the _____, a skillful warrior. 25:27
- What does the field represent and who is in control legally (not ultimate control) of the world until Messiah returns? Genesis 3:17, Matthew 13:38 and Ephesians 2:1-2.

- Jacob was a man that _____ in tents. 25:27

- What first came to your mind when you looked at these two men and how they are described (be honest)? If you are like me, I thought that Jacob was a momma's boy and Esau was this rugged, tough dude.

- Would it surprise you to know that dwelling in tents throughout Israelite history, meant that Jacob was a student of God's Word (Torah). He was in the tent gaining wisdom with Grandpa _____ and his father _____.

- The word "quiet" or "plain" in describing Jacob, could be translated upright or undefiled in Hebrew.
- Esau is the firstborn of two sons, so the inheritance will be divided 2/3 for Esau and _____ for Jacob (Esau's birthright as firstborn).
- Esau sells his entire _____ for a bowl of stew (or soup). 25:29-34. Are you thinking that either Esau really has his priorities out of order or that was some really good stew? No food is worth trading your birthright away.
- Esau gave away his physical belongings (birthright) of being the _____ son. 25:25, 34.

8. Covenant is continued with Isaac. 26:5

- Isaac was the firstborn spiritually, but not physically?   T or F (Genesis 15:3-5, 21:12)
- Covenant is confirmed with Isaac because of the obedience of _____. 26:5, 25.
- What does Isaac do in verse 25? What does this mean again? Lesson 5 Number 6.

9. Isaac is _____ now and it is time to _____ the firstborn son. 27:1-4.

- ❖ **Blessing** (*b'rakah or barak* in Hebrew)- to present a gift or to give honor to another. [9] Blessing someone is to speak life and truth into them so they may walk in righteousness and serve the Righteous and Almighty God. This is not to be confused with positive thinking as if it is about you. This is about God. Many parents, including myself, bless their children by speaking the truth that they are in a Godly family and they have the privilege to carry the next generation forward in fear and obedience to their Creator. Blessings come to those that walk in obedience and curses come to those that walk in disobedience. Deuteronomy chapter 28, Psalm 1:1-3, Proverbs 11:11, Matthew 5:5-13.

- Rebekah hears that _____ wants to bless his oldest son and she calls _____ so that he may receive the blessing. 27:5-13.
- Rebekah tells Jacob to go take the blessing in 27:14-29. T or F
- _____ is blessed by Isaac right before _____ comes in. 27:30

10. Why did Rebekah tell Jacob to purposefully deceive his father? 25:22-23.

- What was the bigger plan behind what Rebekah was doing?

- How do the events that are found in the following scriptures help you understand why Rebekah did what she did? 25:23, 33, 27:41, 28:8-9.Romans 9:13, Malachi 1:2.

- Remember there are only two kinds of people as you have learned—those that are

    _____ and those that are _____What kind of man

    was Esau?

➢ Is this about "the end justifies the means" or is it about doing what is righteous and protecting the righteous, even though the method may seem wrong at the moment? Did Jacob act in deception or obedience? (Remember the line to the Messiah. 25:22-23, 26:5)

- ▪ **Illustration**: A man is abusive to his children and you are aware of what has been happening. The father is drunk and comes to your house and asks if the children are there. You "lie" (chose love and life) and say no. You "lied" to protect the innocent, thus doing what is righteous. This is not "the end justifies the means" but walking in righteousness. Thus, you would not be lying.

11. Jacob marries _____, but he thought he was marrying _____? Genesis 29:15-23.

- ❖ **Definitive Thought**: In the ANE (Ancient Near East—cultural setting), the firstborn daughter was to be married before the second born daughter, thus Laban was actually doing the right thing and Jacob would have known this. Can you think of any things in our culture that are right, but you prefer your way instead?

- He was tricked by Laban, who was his own _____.
- Jacob _____ with the man of the LORD. Genesis 32:28, Hosea 12:3-4.
  ➢ Did Jacob actually have the power to beat up the man sent by God? Was that the point? Wrestling with God represents your salvation and your sanctification (your journey). As you learned in the introduction, salvation is not about one day, but a lifetime of walking in obedience. It is part of your journey. There is even more to this when it comes to Jacob's life right now. Keep going.

- Jacob was wrestling for his _____. 32:26-29
- Didn't he already have his _____? 27:30
- Was that _____ received in the normal fashion? He knew he needed to be properly blessed, not just by man, but by the hand of God.

12. Jacob's name is changed to _____. 32:28, 35:10.

- What does God say to Israel that he also said to Abraham and Isaac? See 12:1, 26:3.

A. Memory Verse: Genesis 32:28, Write it here.

B. Six questions to ask while thinking back through the text.

1. Who are the two main characters?

2. What is the biggest difference between them?

3. When do you see the character or behavioral differences?

4. Where does Rebekah get her important information?

5. Why is it important to listen to God as Rebekah did?

6. How would this have turned out if Rebekah made another choice?

C. Application How does this biblical truth affect how I live my life each day?

D. Journal and prayer time. Is there a sin you need to confess? As you do this, ask God to help you live according to what you have just studied. Praise Him for His wonderful promises to you.

Lesson 7: Jacob and His Sons (12 tribes of Israel)

You may be asking if you will ever get out of the first book of the bible and the answer is yes. This is the last lesson in Genesis. The reason that I will have you spend so much time in the first 5 books of the bible is that this is the foundation of your faith journey that you have begun. When building a house, the foundation is the most important part of the building project. As I stated in the introduction, it is important to know the biblical history and it begins with the first book. This way, you will get a correct view of Scripture and you will not try to skip ahead and thus learn about God incorrectly. I can assure you that millions have tried to learn the "beginning from the end" but the bible states that to truly understand God's message of salvation, you need to know that God has declared "the end from the beginning." See Isaiah 46:10 and 40:21-22 for example.

1. Jacob has _____ children by two different wives? Genesis 29:31-30:24, 35:18

- Rachel and her servant conceived (had) _____ children.

- Leah and her servant conceived _____ children.

2. Israel (Jacob) loved _____ more than any of his other sons because he was the son of his _____age. Genesis 37:3

- Israel made him a _____, representing royalty.

- What did his other brothers think of this robe of royalty? 37:4

- Joseph told them his _____. Do you think this helped them like him more or less? 37:5-11.

3. What were the 11 brothers planning to do to Joseph? 37:18-20

- Who stepped in to dissuade (argue against) this idea? What number of child was he in the lineage of Israel? 29:31-32

- The _____is supposed to lead and protect the family.

- In 37:22, Reuben suggested they shed no _____, but cast him into the pit.

- Who did they sell him to in 37:25?

- Who is this people group (Genesis 16:11)? _____ This means he is Jacob's _____, thus they were family.

- What was Reuben's reaction when he found the pit was empty? 37:29

- The "tearing of garments" meant that you recognized something unrighteous had taken place against God.
- Joseph was sold to the Midianites and then to Potiphar in _____ 37:36

4. Who did Joseph claim was responsible for all of his success? 39:3-4

- In 39:3-4, the blessings on Joseph were noticeable to those around him? T or F

- Joseph was given position of _____ and was in charge of _____ that he had. 39:4

5. Joseph had it going on and apparently this caught the eye of Potiphar's _____. 39:6-7

- What kind of man is Joseph? 39:6-10

- Joseph examined the situation and acted according to what was right (righteous). He did not go for the temporary fulfillment or fix, but instead realized that he was blessed by God and walked in the fear of God. Proverbs 1:7, 9:10.

- ❖ **Righteousness defined** (*tsaddikah or tsaddik*)- literally means straight or one who walks in a straight line; also what is just or lawful. [10] God determines what is straight and what is crooked or what is righteous and what is unrighteous. God wrote the law according to His character and nature, and thus what is right emanates (comes from or out of) from the character and nature of God. To walk in righteousness does not mean you will walk in perfection or without sin.

- **Illustration:** Have you ever heard the saying, "the grass always looks greener on the other side?" The problem is when you get to the other side, the grass you just left looks pretty green and nice. Satan will always make it seem like you need something more or life will be better if you just have a nicer car, a nicer cell phone, etc. Focus on the purpose of what you need and not get caught up in "needing" something else. The purpose of a phone is for communication and certain other necessities, but not every feature is needed. Facebook is a great tool for reconnecting with old friends and family members, as well as a tool for socializing, keeping in contact and sharing ideas, thoughts, but this tool can become an obsession that keeps you caught up in the moment or living a fantasy life, which leads you away from your higher purposes each day. Remember this when you go to make choices each day. What do you really need to buy or do each day? Be content and walk in righteousness.

6. God gave him _____ with the prison warden (keeper) just as he did with Potiphar. 39:4, 21.

7. When the chief cupbearer and baker had dreams, who does God point to in order to interpret the dreams? 40:1-5

- He interpreted their dreams and the chief cupbearer did not _____ Joseph. 40:23
- After _____ years in prison, Pharaoh has a dream. Now the cupbearer _____ Joseph. 41:1-10
- Joseph tells Pharaoh that interpretations are from _____. 40:8, 41:16.
- After Joseph interprets the dreams he puts him over _____ of his house. 41:38-40.

   Again God blesses Joseph.

- Look at Joseph's life and think about being <u>blessed</u>. His brothers plotted to kill him, he is thrown into a pit, sold into slavery 3 times, falsely accused, put into prison, and left in prison. Does this sound blessed?

- **Definitive Thought: Honor and Shame**—If you look at what Joseph has been through, you see what looks like a pretty tough life, by most definitions. However, we see an incredible God restore Joseph from a place of shame to a place of honor. Do you realize that if you are saved, then you have come from shame to honor? This is important to understand. As you look at this idea of restoring you from a place of sinfulness or shame, to a place of restoration or honor, thank God for where you are now. Also, never forget that any time you have been shamed, God can bring you to a place of honor if you will trust (have faith) in Him. And ultimately, eternal life will be the ultimate honor given by our King. Shame will be remembered no more!

- Blessings only come from _____ to God, so would you say Joseph is blessed? Does blessing mean that things only go just as you want them to? Discuss this with someone that is also doing this curriculum and see what they think as well.

8. Joseph has two sons named _____ and _____ 41:50-52.

9. Jacob sends his sons to Egypt to buy _____ so they may _____. 42:2

10. What happens in Genesis 42:6? Look back at 37:7-10

- Joseph _____ his brothers but they did not recognize him. 42:8

- Joseph tests his _____ in chapters 42-44 to see if they have changed.

11. Joseph makes himself known to his _____. 45:1

- What is the first question he asks his brothers in 45:3?

- Joseph tells his brothers not to be distressed or angry with himself because you sold me here, as God sent me before you to preserve _____. 45:5.

12. _____ comes to Egypt with his family and they settle in _____. 46:1-3, 47:1.

13. Israel (Jacob) is about to die and he must _____ Joseph's sons. 48:9

- Israel says, "And now your two sons are _____." 48:5

- Name the two reasons that Jacob did not recognize Ephraim and Manasseh. 48:5, 10.

- Does the reason given in verse 10 remind you of an earlier event? 27:24-26, 30.

- Jacob knew that he had done the right thing, but it was still difficult to do and now he gets to bless his _____ as if they are his own. 48:9

14. Joseph brings the boys to Jacob the way he knew they were to be blessed, according to who was the firstborn and this was _____. 48:12-20.

- Jacob switches them and blesses _____ first and says, "his offspring will become a multitude of nations" or the "fullness of the Gentiles." See Romans 11:25

15. Chapter 49 is prophetic and speaks about will happen to each of the twelve tribes.

- _____ is a lions cub…..The scepter shall not depart from Judah. Psalm 68:78, Psalm 108:8, Hebrews 1:8.

- Who comes from the tribe of Judah? Hebrews 7:14, Rev 5:5

16. When Joseph's brothers came to ask for forgiveness, Joseph tells them "As for you, you meant _____ against me, but God meant it for _____. 50:15-20.

> **Extreme Thought: Injustice-** When you look at each day, each month and each year of your life, remember that there are injustices that will come into your life, things that you don't understand and you will say "that is not fair" or "why does he/she seem to have it all in life? Have you ever said that life is unfair or why does it seem like he/she gets all the breaks and my life stinks. I want you to know the absolute truth that you are not the only one that has felt this way, and in fact if you were to share this struggle with your parents and friends, you will be surprised to find you are far from alone on these issues. Think of Joseph and all that he went through. The very things that could be or are evil, God can work out if you trust and obey Him just like Joseph did. God is still in control (sovereign). Ephesians 1:11

> **Extreme Thought: Honoring Parents-** Some of you may have just read my suggestion to talk with your parents and some of you know that your relationship with your parents is not what it should be, to say the least. I do not know your individual situation, so I can't tell you exactly what to do in your particular situation. However, I can say that God tells you to obey your parents (Ephesians 6:1) and to honor your parents (Exodus 20:12), so pray for your relationship to be one in which you can honor them, and they can trust you. I was like most people, who did not always honor my parents, and I often put my friends before my parents. Does anyone know why this makes no sense besides what I just told you from the bible? My parents will always be my parents that God gave me, but I only have 1-2 friends that were my friends when I was in high school. I pray that you make this a priority in life, or you will have some regrets about it later, as I did.

A. Memory Verse: Genesis 50:20, Write it here.

B. Six questions to ask while thinking back through the text.

1. Who is the main character?

2. What did he do that got him in so much family trouble?

3. When do you see his character come out?

4. Where does Joseph end up?

5. Why was this location important for the future of their family?

6. How did Joseph see things differently than his brothers did?

C. Application How does this biblical truth affect how I live my life each day? Does this explain what you see in the news each day or what you see in your family and friends?

D. Journal and prayer time. Is there a sin you need to confess? As you do this, ask God to help you live according to what you have just studied. Praise God for his goodness.

Lesson 8: Salvation in the Exodus (A Nation Gets Their Identity)

Read Exodus chapters 1-14. I don't know if you realize this yet, but each time you learn a memory verse, you are doing a history lesson. See, each memory verse places you at a different time in history. So when someone asks you one day to give them a summary of the history of the biblical times, your 30+ memory verses will be a great way to answer. You can teach your parents, family members or even your children one day, through these verses. If you have gotten behind and can't remember the memory verse for lesson 2 or 5 or any other chapter, it is not too late to memorize it and get your history back in order. Go back to the beginning and look at my suggestions on memorizing scripture and get right back on track.

Okay, lesson 7 left you with Joseph as the second in command in Egypt, Joseph's family is all doing well and Jacob was even able to bless his grandsons as his own. They all lived happily ever after. Well, I would like to tell you this is what happened, but things take a different turn in history. Are you ready to see God's salvation and power at work? I know sometimes you may look at how much there is to read, and be a little concerned, but that is okay. Do your best before God and pray that He gives you a desire to want to read more than ever before. He will listen to His child. You are His child if you have received His salvation.

1. What were Joseph's last words to his brothers? Genesis 50:24-26

2. What changed from Joseph's rule as governor in Genesis? Exodus 1:8-11

The command is given by Pharaoh to kill each_____ _____ born to the Hebrews, 1:15-22, 2:11

- Did the midwives obey Pharaoh or God? Did they lie and why was it okay here? 1:15-20 (see Lesson 6 #7-8)

- Who survived because of the midwives' decision? Exodus 2:1-10

- Who ends up nursing Moses? God has a plan doesn't He?

3. Moses has to leave because he _____ an Egyptian. Exodus 2:12-14

- _____ fled Egypt and ends up in Midian and marries Zipporah. 2:16-22.

- In 2:23-24, the Israelites cry out and God remembers His _____ with _____, _____ and Jacob.

4. Moses has an encounter with a _____ bush, and finds out that he is in the presence of the _____ of Abraham, Isaac and Jacob. 3:1-6

- When you come into the presence of God that place is always _____.
- What promise did he speak to Moses? 3:8, See Genesis 15:18-20, 50:24-25.

- God is ready to _____ His people with an outstretched arm. 6:6
  - ❖ **Redeem defined** (*Gaal* in Hebrew)- To buy back, to bring someone back around in order to restore or deliver them. [11] God bought us from being slaves to sin to slaves to righteousness, through the blood of Yeshua. See Exo. 6:6, Isaiah 44:24, Galatians 4:5.

  - ❖ **Slavery defined in the Bible-** What is your current picture of slavery that just entered your mind? This is most likely not God's definition. Slavery was a vibrant part of society as many could only work by being slaves to someone. However, slaves were not treated horribly in most cases, but often were treated so well that they wanted to stay even when their time was up, thus becoming extended family.

- What does God call his people in 3:9?

  - ➢ Was Moses ready to go and free the people? 3:11, 4:11-13. Will you be ready to go when God calls or will you find excuses like Moses did? Go back to Genesis 1:1- "In the beginning, God created the heavens and earth." If you believe this, then trusting God to take care of you is a small thing. God's got you covered!

5. How does God answer when Moses asks Him to give him a name that he can tell the Hebrews? He says "I _____ Who I _____! 3:14

  - ❖ **"I AM" defined-** You can read volumes about this, but here is my humble explanation of this term. God is saying that I don't have to explain myself nor would you understand everything if I did. I have always been here and I will always be here. I am absolutely independent of man and my creation. I am consistent in all that I do and I see all and know all. This Name defines me yet I am un-definable. However God does help to define Himself in the sense that He says, "I am the "God of your fathers, the God of

Abraham, Isaac, and Jacob." I am always to be associated with my people that I have chosen and I will never forget my covenant with all who will receive my salvation because my character cannot do so. This separates Him from all other gods because He is a God of relationships.

❖ <u>What is your new name?</u> The Hebrew word for name is *shem* and also means reputation or renown. [12] When you say someone has a good reputation, you come to this conclusion based on what they do, not just what they say. God's name is what He does and thus who He is as God. If you are a child of God, your name is changed to be His child and thus you are to walk in the name, the reputation of God revealed in different ways, including revelation through Jesus the Christ. Read Galatians 2:20, Acts 4:18, 2 Corinthians 5:17, Psalm 145:2

- God can only do that which agrees with His character and nature and so each time He reveals one of His names, they reveal more about His character and nature.

  ➢ In Genesis 18:25, it says that God is _____. Do you think God has to try to be this way or will He always do this because that is who He is (I AM WHO I AM)?

6. Pharaoh is about to meet God and God knows the _____ of Pharaoh because of what He says in 3:18-20. God knows what is in Pharaoh and He also knows the future. 3:21-22.

- There is a battle going on between God and Pharaoh (self-proclaimed god). Look at the following verses to see the issue of "hardening of the heart." Who does the hardening in each of the verses listed? 4:21, 7:3, 14, 22, 8:19, 32, 9:7, 12, 10:1, 20, 27, 11:10, 14:4.

- Was it right that God hardened Pharaoh's heart because this means he could not choose what is good, but only evil? Look back at 3:19.

  ▪ **Illustration**: The same sun that melts the wax also hardens the clay. God already knew the condition of his heart. God just revealed it to everyone by testing Pharaoh the way He did. Pharaoh thought that he was a god, so Moses was saying, in a sense, my God can beat up your god. Exodus 14:4, 18

    ➢ **Extreme Thought:** As you grow in the LORD, and God wants you to grow in him, how does He do this? For example, if God wants you to control the words that come out of your mouth, will he just force you speak nicer the next day or will he give you opportunities with other people and see how you respond? Will you be looking for God at work now?

7. List the 10 plagues. 7:14-12:32. Time to read; it is good stuff!

8. In Chapter 12, God is about to do something so big in history that he tells them to set their calendar by this event. It shall be the _____ of months, the first of Aviv (Nisan).

- On the 10th day, each man shall take a _____ without _____ 12:3-5.
- He shall keep it until the _____ day and then sacrifice it, take the _____ and put it on the side posts and the upper doorpost. See Lesson 2, Number 15.
- God is coming to covenant with his people. Can God break the covenant? Go back to lesson 5 number 8 (Genesis 15).

  ❖ **Covenant defined-** it is a binding agreement between two or more parties (usually 2) through the sacrifice of an unblemished animal, which is cut into two pieces and split so that the blood covered the space between the two sides. Then the two parties, with backs to one another walked through in a figure 8 until they faced each other. <u>Then they agreed to the terms of the covenant and by doing so they were saying that if either of us breaks this agreement, might death come to us just as it came to that animal.</u> You can compare it to a modern-day contract, but the penalty for breaking it was much more serious than our current judicial system with its many loopholes, etc. In relationship to this was a threshold covenant (seen here in Exodus 12), which is still practiced in many nations today. When you entered a home and you stepped over the threshold, you were entering into covenant with that person or family, including covenant with their God or gods (some still sacrifice right there at the front door so the blood spills on the threshold). If you entered the front door without any concern for covenant, you were saying that you want to bring harm to this family and you do not care about how they live in their home.

  ➢ After you read this definition, do you understand why it is so serious to God when you break His covenant by disobeying His commands? He can and will forgive you when you repent, but you are to walk in obedience to the only God who saved you.

9. Let's look at this covenant in the Passover- see 8 above.

- God offers salvation, if they will receive it on His terms. _____ is coming to destroy the wickedness of Egypt and all who agree with this system. Exodus 12:12.

- In Exodus 12:13, there is a sign of the covenant which is the _____ .

- God establishes a _____ with them in 12:13, 23, as he passes over the threshold or into their houses. The _____ on the doorposts said two things—I obey you and you are welcome in this place to covenant with us. Wow!

- God says that you shall keep this day of Passover as a statute or command _____ . 12:14

- God says that you shall keep the Feast of _____ bread as a statute forever. 12:17. How long is forever?

- How many households were affected by the LORD's promise to kill the firstborn of those that would not obey Him? 12:29

10. The Exodus begins and how many people left? Were they all Israelites? 12:33-38

- God has only one _____ for the _____ and the _____ (made up of Egyptians and other slave nations that were in Egypt). 12:49

- God will guide them by a pillar of _____ by day and a pillar of _____ by night. 13: 21-22.

  ➤ Take a moment and read Chapter 14. Does the suspense and drama remind you of any movies you have seen lately? How would you do this if you were the director? Just a thought to help you get a visual and now back to the questions.

- Were the people trusting God? Did they forget what he had done? 14:11-14

- How did they get across the sea?

- Who won the battle? Did God save his people? 14:27-30

11. I want you to take a snapshot of what you have just seen in Exodus so far. You have seen a picture of salvation. I want to expound a little more so you know how good God is throughout all of history. Notice that I did not wait until they enter the Promised Land to declare the concept of salvation. In other words, people are "saved", but they still have a journey of life left ahead of them. Sound familiar? The Promised Land is not synonymous with spending eternity with God, but it acts as a type and shadow of salvation. After all, Moses had God's salvation, but he did not enter the Promised Land. Do not ever believe that your salvation can be summarized by a moment in time. Look at verses like Philippians 2:12, 1 Corinthians 15:1-2—"are being saved."

- As you notice, I will occasionally put in a Hebrew definition. Hebrew is the language that most of the Old Testament is written in and so much of the New Testament's (NT) terms began from the Old Testament (OT), not to mention how many verses in the NT are quotes from the OT. This is the reason I will refer to some Hebrew words from time to time.

- In 14:13, the English bible says "fear not, stand firm, and see the salvation of the LORD, which he will work for you today." The word "salvation" in Hebrew is y'shua. Jesus in Hebrew is Y'shua (some pronounce it Yeshua) which means to rescue or deliver from trouble and restored back to God; also means salvation or God is salvation.

- Y'shua is made up of 3 Hebrew consonant letters, like the majority of Hebrew words.

  ✓ Y'shua is made up of a yod, shin and ayin
  ✓ Yod is a picture of a hand and means a deed or action
  ✓ Shin is a picture of teeth and means to destroy or consume.
  ✓ Ayin is a picture of an eye and means to cast your eyes or to look upon.
  ✓ Picture of Y'shua (salvation)- It begins with action or a rescue, followed by the destruction of the thing you were rescued from, and then ended by devotion to or casting your eyes upon that which delivered you.
  ✓ The Israelites were rescued, the enemy was destroyed, they walked through the water (baptism) and they cast their devotion and eyes upon the LORD. Exodus 1-15.

A. Memory Verse: Exodus 6:3-4, Write it out here.

B. Six questions to ask while thinking back through the text.

1. Who is in control?

2. What is Jesus' Hebrew name and what does it mean?

3. When was Pharaoh's heart hardened?

4. Where were the Israelites taken from?

5. Why did they need to get out of Egypt (spiritually)?

6. How did God take them out? Exodus 6:6

C. Application How does this biblical truth affect how I live my life each day?

D. Journal and prayer time. Is there a sin you need to confess? As you do this, ask God to help you live according to what you just studied. Praise God for miracles still today.

Lesson 9: Promised Land: Here We Come (Exodus)

Do you recall when God promised Abram that he would inherit the land? Well, it is time for the descendants of Abram to go and take it. As you go through the book of Exodus, remember this is what they are supposed to do. Are you ready to see what happens next? As the sections of scripture get larger, it will get tougher to read all of the chapters. I encourage you to read as much as you can. Just because it is more, please do not be tempted to skip reading except for the few verses to answer your questions. This will still be okay, but take the high road and do as much as you can. After all, you have a full 2 weeks to do each lesson if you are doing it as a year-long study. Read as much as you can and you will be surprised what you learn on your own.

Think about something for one moment. The Bible is the character and nature of God revealed to mankind, so doesn't it make sense to read about God to learn about God to live for God? No one is keeping score, but God wants you to know Him and have a relationship with you just like you want to know and have a good relationship with your spouse and children. You know your Father, your Creator, by reading His Word and obeying it! Read Exodus 15-40 if you are able. Before beginning this lesson, at least read through chapter 21.

1. The people _____ against Moses, saying what shall we drink? Exodus 15:2

- In Exodus 16:2-4, they now grumble because they have no _____. So God says I will send _____ from heaven.

2. God teaches the people about the Sabbath, a day of restoration or renewal. 16:22-23

- It is to be a _____ day. 16:23, also read Genesis 2:3.
  ➢ How long are you to obey the Sabbath and keep it holy? What day is the Sabbath and has it changed? Genesis 2:3, Exodus 31:16, Isaiah 66:23, Hebrews 4:10-12. Over the years, people named the days of the week (Google and see the pagan connection). It used to be Day 1, Day 2, Day 3, Day 4, Day 5, Day 6, Shabbat (Sabbath)—Gen. 1 gives us this pattern. Man's sin has infected our entire world in certain ways.

- God tested them and did they listen? 16:4-5, 20-21.
- What was the test? 16:20-27

➤ **Sabbath:** A word picture associated with renewal just as a new moon each month is the renewal of things for every 30 day cycle. God gave us this renewal and restoration time each week and shows us each month as we see the slightest sliver of the moon each month. You live in the busiest culture ever. Will you give God 24 hours every Sabbath (Saturday) to meet with and rest in Him, physically, emotionally and spiritually? Some believe that we are to follow the lunar calendar and some say we should follow the solar calendar. God's calendar is a combination of the two calendars as well as an agricultural calendar. See Genesis 1 for the description of a day. Shabbat (Sabbath) begins Friday night at sunset and goes to sunset on Saturday. Days in the bible and Israel still today go from sunset to sunset. How could the Sabbath change your life?

- Do you remember why you should obey God? When you obey you are _____. Deuteronomy 28

  ➤ In 17:3, the people grumbled about having no water again. 17:3. Do you see a pattern here? Are there things that you continually grumble or complain about? Is it with your mom, dad, siblings, boss or teachers? Read Philippians 2:14 before you answer this. Write down some thoughts and pray about them.

3. Read chapter 19 right now. It is an awesome scene. In Exodus 19:5, God says, "Now therefore _____you will obey my voice and keep my _____ you shall be my treasured possession among all the peoples, for all the earth is mine." Psalm 24:1

- The people responded and said, "_____ that the LORD has spoken we will do." 19:8
- What is about to happen? They are coming to _____God. 19:17
- Can you approach God anyway you want? Psalm 24:1-4

- Does God test us at times? 20:20, 16:4.

➢ What does a test teach us about our heart, our motives?

4. God gives the 10 commandments to the people. There are 613 commandments of God but God is going to just give them ten for now, in writing. Do not get hung up on the fact that 613 is a large number because you are already obeying many of them and do not even know it. You will learn more as you walk down this journey. Let's look at the 10 commandments for now.

✓ You shall have no other _____ _____ _____. 20:3

✓ You shall not make for yourself a _____ _____ (idols). 20:4

✓ You shall not take the _____ of the LORD your God in _____ (to make worthless or common). 20:7 (Also go back to Lesson 7 #5 concerning "name")

✓ Remember the Sabbath and keep it _____. 20:8

✓ Honor your _____ and _____ (all the time not just when you feel like it). 20:12

✓ You shall not _____. 20:13, Matthew 5:21-22

✓ You shall not commit _____. 20:14, Matthew 5:27

✓ You shall not _____l. 20:15

✓ You shall not bear _____ witness (shall not lie). 20:16

✓ You shall not _____ (desire what is not yours to be yours), 20:17

➢ Do you think these are some good truths to live by? I want you to take some time to discuss these with someone else so that you can check your obedience in these areas. Write down the one that you struggle with the most right now.

5. Did you notice that God asks them to keep his covenant before he lays out all the things they are supposed to do?

➢ You may be thinking that this is not fair and God should be up front with me. Actually God is saying that obeying my commands is not what saves you, but after you come to faith by my grace, then you will obey me. You see this laid out in Ephesians 2:1-10. Your response to God will be obedience. <u>Isn't it great that entering into covenant (salvation) does not depend upon our own ability to do what is right</u>?

6. The covenant is confirmed between God and the people. 24:1-8. How did they respond this time? Refer back to 19:8

7. In Exodus 25:8, you will see what the next few chapters are about: "And let them make me a tabernacle, that I may dwell in their midst."

- Did God dwell with Adam and Eve without a house or dwelling place?
- What happened to change this?

8. What did God try to do in Exodus 19 and 20? How did the people respond? 20:20

- Instead of the close intimate relationship like in the Garden of Eden and later in Acts chapter 2, God will now appear in a building to dwell with them. See a difference?

➢ I will be impressed if you read Exodus chapters 25-30, because I would probably not have done so at your age. However, if you take the challenge to do so, I would like you to look at the instructions for building the temple and take notice of how God does this. How does this make you feel about your relationship with God after reading this, considering you are called a priest and your body is the temple of the Spirit of God?

9. The one thing I am asking you to do for this portion is to look up in your bible and you can also go to **www.templeinstitute.org and** get the details and pictures of the temple and the priest's garments. In future studies, you can look at the deeper meaning.

- Priests could not just approach the service of God according to their own ways, but must come in purity and be completely clean, even down to the clothes they wore to honor God, (Exodus 29:21, Psalm 24:4).

- Priests were to guard the temple, the people and the Torah (instructions, words of God). You will see this some through your studies.

  - ➢ Did you know that all true believers are called priests before God? This is not exactly the same because there is no temple and will not be one until Jesus returns, but you are to live with purity and walk in holiness before a holy God, (1 Peter 2:5, 9). God the Father is to be approached in certain ways still today. God will restore what was lost by the people's decision to forfeit their calling to be priests (Exodus 19:6, 20:19-21)

  - ❖ **Extreme Thought: A Father's Love-** Are you struggling with the concept of a loving father, because you do not, nor ever had a good relationship with your earthly father. An earthly father should do certain things for you like spend time with you, give you security, discipline you in order to train you, provide for you, show you proper affection and many other wonderful blessings. For those of you who have never really experienced this, it is not too late to forgive your father and do your best to restore this relationship. If you are unable to do so or if your father has passed away, know that you have a Heavenly Father that provides all the things I listed above and so much more. He is your Creator and knows every detail about you and still loves you. Regardless of what your relationship is with your father, honor him as the Bible says in Ephesians 6. Find comfort in knowing that your Heavenly Father will never leave you nor forsake you. Lastly, view your relationship with your father with the realization that he will never be perfect, but honor him anyway and find things about him to be thankful for. Psalm 68:5

10. Who did the people decide to worship while Moses was up on the mountain meeting with God? Exodus 32:1-5

- How did they decide to worship? 6-10. The term "to play" means the people were having a serious party and anything goes, which would have included open sex and many other lewd acts done in the name of worship. Some of you have seen some movies where the theme was about serious partying. They had nothing on this disgusting party!

- The people were out of the land of Egypt, but much of Egypt was still in their hearts and minds. They were doing what they had seen, and many may have participated in, while in Egypt. They were worshipping the right God in the _____ way because they referred to him as Yehovah (YHWH) in 32:5.

- What did God tell Moses in 32:10? Was God angry or what? (it is okay to have righteous anger).

➢ What does God refer back to in 32:13-14? Was God planning on changing His covenant (promise) or was he just going to do this with new descendants of Moses?

- How did Moses respond to this crazy party? 32:19

- What were the consequences for disobedience? 32:20-30, 35.

- What happened in their relationship and what caused it? 33:3

11. Moses intercedes (goes between them and God) for the people.
    - In 33:13, Moses wants to find favor (grace) and to find favor, he says, "show me your

      _____ that I may _____ you. When you think that reading and studying your

      Bible (Word of God), is not important, **remember that this is how you find favor with**

      God and know God.

12. Look at 33:3 and compare to 33:15.
    - How did Moses feel about going anywhere without God?

      ➢ What will your life look like now and for eternity if you go without God?

13. In chapters 35-40, Moses follows the directions earlier and builds the tabernacle. Now that

the tabernacle is built, the _____ of the LORD filled it. And _____ was

not able to go in. 40:35.

A. Memory Verse: Exodus 34:6, Write it out here.

B. Six questions to ask while thinking back through the text:

1. Who missed out on intimate relationship with God as Moses did?

2. What did they need to do for this relationship?

3. When did Moses realize what was happening with the calf?

4. Where was Moses when the party was going on?

5. Why did they fail to have this kind of relationship with God?

6. How did God dwell with them after this?

C. Application How does this biblical truth affect me each day?

D. Journal and prayer time. Is there a sin you need to confess? As you do this, ask God to help you live according to what you have studied. Praise God that you are called priests before Him; what a privilege! May we walk in holiness to our God.

Lesson 10: God is Holy; Man is Sinful—What Can Man Do?   (Book of Leviticus)

You have made it to lesson 10. **Yes!** This lesson will be a little tough to grasp in some ways because you live in a culture that has labeled you as a teenager. Did you know that this word did not even exist until 1941? So in the years following 1941, instead of being a child and then an adult, you were now a teenager. With this label has come the cultural ideology that you can live **without <u>responsibility</u>, <u>accountability (objective morality)</u>, or <u>respect</u>.** This is a formula for a me-centered selfish life. You can just "somehow" grow up and become an "adult" without these three things. If you think I am exaggerating, it may be because you have bought into this label of behavior. I do not say this to be harsh, but it has been my experience that at least half of the "teens" I meet see things this way. Many do not realize it until given a different perspective.

 I am asking you to think about these 3 words that are bolded above as you enter this book and think about living before a holy God who calls His children to live holy *(be set apart).* These 3 words are key words for any nation or group of people to co-exist with one another without chaos and extreme immorality. If you can display these words with those you meet everyday, then you can do the same before a holy God. If you have no respect for authority on Earth, you will not respect the Creator of the Earth (God Almighty). Part of the idea of holiness is to *be set apart* in a world that wants to define you and teach you its worldview.

The book of Leviticus speaks about some very serious things in our relationship with our Creator, and thus how to live for Him each day? Leviticus is not about instant gratification, short google articles or youtube videos. Leviticus is about living before a holy God each day and *taking the time* to find out how to live for and approach the Creator of the Universe, who is so powerful and loving at the same time. He is calling His children into relationship with Him. The book of Leviticus can also be a tough read because there is so much detail, containing so many of God's perfect laws but remember God loved you enough to give you these laws (not all are for us today but many are directly or indirectly). So read what you can and as you go through this lesson, I will make it a little easier to understand. In Jerusalem to this day, young Jewish boys at age 4-5 begin studying the Scriptures, and the first book they study is Leviticus. So if you get discouraged or think you cannot do it, remember there are 5 year olds doing this right now. Okay, you never stop learning until you die, and I know you are not dead yet, so let's go!

1. At the end of Exodus, God's presence came to dwell in the camp inside the tabernacle, but the people, cannot go in. Why could they not just come in anytime they wanted and however they wanted? Exodus 33:3, 20.

2. Leviticus centers upon the holiness of God and the sinfulness and dependence upon God found in man. So how can you draw near to God so you may worship Him?
    *   God is holy so He is dangerous? You may ask yourself why is He dangerous? He is

        _____ and man is _____. This is dangerous!

- Why does it matter if man can't go into the tabernacle? Who is in there?

- The one place you always want to be is in the presence of the _____!

  - **Illustration**: Imagine you are at a power plant, and there is a huge grid with mega wattage, and you pry open the door and just walk in. Zap, you are dead. This is what happens when ultimate goodness and sin cross one another. Sin cannot enter where He dwells, and the radiance of His glory will ultimately destroy you. God is not out to get us, but our sin separates us from God and can destroy our relationship with Him and thus destroys other relationships here on earth. Allow him to reveal whom He is and that He wants to be near you. We must approach Him on His terms.

  - ❖ **Holiness (of God) defined** (*Kadosh* in Hebrew)- One who is set apart as special. He is not like that which He created, but is different, above, separate, and yet He relates to His creation out of love and revelation. [13]

- In Leviticus 1:1-7, approaching God was possible by bringing an _____or Korban in Hebrew. This term means "as brought near to another" so the animal is what you bring when you are drawing near to the LORD. [14]

- As you are reading verses 1-7, does it remind you of entering into a blood covenant? Genesis 15:12-17 and read Hebrews 9:22, 10:4.

- **Critical Thought: Bringing Sacrifices To The Temple**. A holy God is in the tabernacle and sinful and dependent man wants to draw near. There are different types of offerings, but the idea centers on drawing near to God. Not all offerings are about sin. However man is sinful, which means some sins are intentional or in rebellion and others are unintentional, but either type separates you from God. Every time you desire to draw near to God, you need to be cleansed or atoned (sins forgiven). Otherwise, you cannot approach a holy God. The offerings (sacrifices) could not bring forgiveness of your sins, because an animal has no power to forgive sins, and neither did the priest, but they were the way by which God allowed you to draw near, ultimately looking forward to the day when Yeshua would be the high priest and the offering that would be made "once for all." (Hebrews 7:27, 9:12, Romans 6:10). So the priests were given the authority by God to intercede for the people. As someone would come with a repentant heart, the spotless sacrifice was accepted, and their sins were forgiven or their sacrificed was accepted, dependent upon what sacrifice they were bringing. Remember, not all sacrifices were for sins, but man is tainted with sin, whether intentional or unintentional. **Without a repentant heart, no one may approach God, no matter how many sacrifices you brought.** Remember this truth when you approach God each day. God gives you the way and means to draw near but repentance is the key to entering into the presence of God in salvation and each day as you continue to walk in salvation until your Redeemer and Great high Priest (Yeshua) returns. Read Hebrews chapters 7-8 to understand that Yeshua was and is always the way to draw near to the Father. After all, He was the only one who perfectly obeyed the laws of God!

> ➢ **Extreme Thought!** Who takes the animal and cuts its throat on some of these sacrifices? Have you ever killed an animal up close? If you had to kill an animal and realize that symbolically, the animal took your place, wouldn't this make you think about how you lived your life? Yeshua did this for you as he took your place! Stop right now and thank Him for doing this for you!

❖ **Atonement defined** (*Kafar* in Hebrew)- In its earliest Hebrew form, it is a picture of a village or a lion, meaning protection. When you are atoned, you are protected, thus you can approach God. It also means to cover or to reconcile. [15] Therefore, coming in repentance and obedience keeps you protected and reconciled to God. Otherwise, you are outside and not with God, who is your protection (2 Corinthians 5:17-21).

❖ **Repentance defined** (Shuv or Nacham in Hebrew)- To turn back to a previous state or place; to be restored back to God. [16] Since you are a descendant of Adam, you want to turn back to the picture of the previous state where there was no sin and to the previous place called the Garden of Eden. When the heavens and earth are restored, things will return to as they were in the Garden. If you just turn from one sin to another, this does you no good. If you are a child of God (disciple of Jesus), you will still struggle with sin until Jesus returns, but your true desire is to live a righteous life that has been declared upon you by God. Righteousness does not mean perfection.

3. So after looking at this, it is not really about death but about _____. Because _____ made a way to allow you to _____ near, you can have life!

4. In Leviticus 8:10, the LORD is _____ Aaron and his sons so they could serve as _____ in the tabernacle. Exodus 29:1

   • In 10:1-3, Aaron's sons Nadab and Abihu offer unauthorized _____ before the LORD and they _____.

   • This happened to them because God is _____ and they acted in _____.

- Some of you may be thinking that this seems a little harsh, but God's natural reaction to any sin is holiness and because he is holy, he must legally bring justice to the sin that has been committed. If it were not for the fact that God is also gracious, every sin we commit would result in death. <u>So with this said, is it right for you to intentionally sin and know that God will just be gracious to you?</u> Explain from what you know so far and see Romans 6:1-2, 15-16.

5. Leviticus chapters 11-22 primarily center upon the theme that you serve a holy God so you are to live a holy life.
   - In chapter 11, God lists what you should and should not _____. Yes, God actually still cares about what you eat today. Would this surprise you since he saved you and calls you his child? God never changes and since he never changes, his laws never change, so you can always believe Him.

   - In Leviticus 19:1-4, (also see 1 Peter 1:16) the LORD tells the people, "You shall be _____ as I the LORD your God is _____. Did you notice the difference in the holiness of God and your holiness as a man?

6. He also gives them 3 commands? Where have you seen these before? Exodus 20. Do you think these are important if God mentions them with the command of being holy?

   ❖ **<u>Holiness (of man) defined</u>** (*Kodesh* in Hebrew, but *Kadosh* if in reference to being like God)- someone that has been separated from the rest for a special purpose; to separate and be joined to God and His ways. [17] It also means that you are to be transparent as God is transparent. This does not mean that we understand all there is to know about God, but it means that God is very clear about His laws, His morality, His truths. If you follow God, your life should be transparent—No Games.

   ▪ **Illustration**: You are walking out of the school after practice and most people are already gone and you find a wallet with no ID in it. It has over $50 in it. You know that your coach is still there, but you have to walk to the side door to get back in. You could wait until the next day. You sure could use that money to pay for some new shoes or some new video games that you have really wanted. <u>Do you walk in holiness?</u>

7. Leviticus 23 mentions 7 appointed times (feasts) or **moedim** in Hebrew. The word means appointed times or purpose set by an authority (God); an appointment or a time that is repeated time after time.[18]

  ➢ This word **moed or plural moedim** is first used in Genesis 1:14 and is usually translated seasons. What does God mean when He uses this word for seasons? Is he simply talking about winter, spring, summer and fall or did he put the moon and sun in the sky for an appointed purpose? Do the sun and moon still do their purpose today? What authority placed them there? Jeremiah 31:35-36 <u>List the 7 appointed times from Leviticus 23 that God asks his people to observe under his authority.</u>

  ➢ Are you supposed to keep the moedim (appointed times) of God still today as part of working out your salvation with fear and trembling? If so, how can you honor these days in obedience to God? You will see later that these appointed times are not like our country's holidays. Holidays usually point to an event or tradition that happened in the past and we are looking back, but with God's appointed times, you are celebrating what happened in the past, what is happening now and what will happen in the future, not to mention fulfilled prophecy on these dates. They are much more exciting than our holidays, although it seems that most people have made man's "holy(i)days" more holy than God's actual holy days. You see that this word is from the beginning in Genesis 1:14, also in Leviticus 23 and then look at the following verses to see what will happen in the future when Jesus returns. Jeremiah 31:35-36, Isaiah 66:23 and Zechariah 14:16-19. You will understand some more when you see the connection between moedim and Yeshua's returns, first and second. Keep studying.

  • **Sabbath**: To make new or restore; to cease for renewal and celebration. You just saw the importance of keeping the Sabbath holy in Leviticus 19 (also see Genesis 2:23, Exodus

16:25, 20:8, 31:14, Isaiah 56, Hebrews 4:8-10) and now it is mentioned as the first of his appointed times in Leviticus 23. Please read the verses about Sabbath. You may be asking the appropriate time for the Sabbath. It is to be observed from Friday at sunset to Saturday at sunset. Biblical time is defined in Genesis 1 and God is still the same as He always has been and will be (See "I AM" in lesson 8).

➢ You may be asking yourself about other people, or maybe yourself, who have to work on Sabbath? How do you honor the Sabbath while at work considering you are supposed to set this day aside as holy; a day of restoration unto God? There is a time when I would have said, don't fret about it because God is grace and it is no problem. However, I came to realize that God does not plan His schedule around me, but vice versa. Do I want to worship Him on His terms, at His holy times or do I want to do it my way. Seek God about what you should do and when you should do it? He will make it clear if you truly seek Him with a sincere heart. Do you have to work on Sabbath or can you get another job? These are choices for you to decide. What we do here matters for all of eternity, as you will learn in later studies. This is not about God being mad at you or about legalism, but about obedience because nothing else is above your relationship with God.

8. Leviticus chapters 24-27 continues with more details about how God's people are to be separate, to live holy lives.

➢ In Leviticus 26:1-27, there is a very important two letter word mentioned 8 times. Hint: Verse 14-15 uses it 3 times and it is _____. So this would tell you that this relationship with God means that we have to ____ something. (grace, pg. 21).

A. **Memory Verse**: Leviticus 19:2

B. <u>Six questions to ask while thinking back through the text</u>.

<u>1. Who has done all things with a purpose?</u>

<u>2. What were the sacrifices for</u>?

<u>3. When were all sins forgiven for that year</u>?

<u>4. Where did God dwell and who could go in there?</u>

<u>5. Why did God give you appointed times?</u>

<u>6. How long are His people to obey them</u>?

C. Application How does this biblical truth affect how I live my life each day?

D. Journal and prayer time. Is there a sin you need to confess and/or a praise to give to God?

Lesson 11: Will The LORD's People Pass His Tests? (Numbers)

The people of God are still going to the Promised Land, but they must go through some tests before getting there. Why do you take tests? It is to see what you have learned. When you pass enough tests, you go to the next grade. Well, God tests His people to see if they have learned how to obey, which is their part of the covenant, in order to be blessed. Otherwise, how can they move forward to the next "grade?" Okay, let's see what God reveals to you next along His biblical truths throughout history. This study covers the entire book of <u>Numbers</u>. It reads like a narrative (story) so read as much as you can. Before you begin, always remember to check the memory verse at the end of the lesson, so you can start memorizing it. Also, take a few minutes and see how many memory verses you can still quote without looking at them. If you cannot do but one or two verses, stop and do this.

Memory verses means you are memorizing, not doing so for one day and forgetting it. If you do this, they will not impact your life and prepare you for spiritual battle when the enemy attacks or when this sinful world gets the best of you. We see the opening chapter with a census of the men from each tribe that are 20 years old to prepare for war, except for the Levites who were taking care and protecting the tabernacle.

1. In Numbers 3:40-41, the Levites replaced the _____males to be redeemed unto God. When did this happen? Exodus 32:28-29

- Was this God's original plan for His people? Exodus 19:5-8

2. In Numbers 5:5-10, it says "When a man or woman commits any of the sins that people commit by breaking faith with the LORD, and that person realizes his guilt, he shall

_____his sin……………and shall make _____ repentance or restitution. Also see 1 John 1:9, James 5:16, Acts 2:38.

- So with this definition of repentance, you can understand why you see the next part. In verse 7, "And he shall make full restitution for his wrong, adding a _____ to it and giving it to him to whom he did the _____."

- The only way to get back to that place of righteousness is to completely restore what you have done. 2 Corinthians 7:10 says, "For Godly grief produces a _____ that leads to salvation without regret, whereas worldly grief produces _____." See it is not just about saying I am sorry and going back to your same old life, but you have a Godly sorrow that will totally restore things.

3. In Numbers 11:1, the people _____ against the LORD and his anger burned among them.

- They were _____because they wanted _____. 11:4. Does this remind you of a pattern that began in Exodus?
- Moses pleads for help from the _____ and he tells Moses to gather _____men of the elders of Israel. 11:13-16, Read Exodus 18:20.
- The people received _____, (11:31) which is what they wanted but there hearts were greedy and ungrateful, so the LORD _____ down the people with a very great _____ 11:32-33.

4. Numbers 12:1-3

- Miriam and Aaron speak against _____, God's appointed prophet.
- Moses was more _____than any other man on the face of the earth. Wow, what a leader he had become!
- God responds to Miriam's words by turning her _____. 12:10. This Hebrew word in the Bible is not leprosy nor Hansen's disease as some think (because this would attach itself even to their clothes and their homes), but a leprous heart (of sin). This sin would manifest itself physically. What happens spiritually often shows up physically just like in our lives today. This is a point so often overlooked in our current churches. The word used here actually means a disease, a mark or affliction given by God.

- ➤ What does this say about gossiping or randomly talking against God's appointed men and women (pastors, teachers, and ministry leaders)?

- They finally made it to the edge of the Promised Land! Let's see what happens next.

5. How many men are sent to check out the land? How many tribes were there? Go back to Genesis 48-49 if you can't remember.

- How many came back with a good report and why were they going in to the land? Give 2 reasons, but the most important is found in Numbers 13:2

- _____ and _____ said "let us go up at once and _____, for we are well able to overcome it. 13:30

- Ten of them said it is a land that _____ its inhabitants, and all the people we saw were very _____, and we seemed to ourselves like _____. 13:31-33.

- In 14:1-4, the people _____against Moses and say, "let us choose a _____and go back to Egypt."

- In verses 5-9, the leaders tell the people, "do not _____ against the LORD and do not fear the people of the land."

➢ Look at this historical truth and think about what happened in Exodus 19-20 at Mt. Sinai. They were about to have this intimate relationship with God and they fear God only as being afraid instead of a real understanding of how to fear God. Proverbs 1:7, 3:7, Psalms 34:7, Proverbs 1:7 says that if you do not fear God you cannot begin to understand Him. This is a fear (I am afraid because of how holy and powerful God is) and a fear of reverence, respect, and awe.

❖ **Extreme Thought**: The question in our culture that is so often repeated is "how can there be so much evil"? We cringe as we are faced with different evils and it scares us to think that we may have to deal with that one day in our own lives. We ask questions like, "How could anyone live through the evil that was done against them?" This is a valid and disturbing question, however, I believe there is a more frightful and disturbing question, "How will I be able to face the absolute goodness of a Holy God? One day I will bring my sinful self to be judged by a good and just God. This fact should shake me daily into giving myself completely to a loving and just God and allowing Him to guide my every thought and deed. The only thing that will save me on that day is that I know there is one God who can save me and He made a way by grace and faith (action) through the Messiah Yeshua. I need to embrace this truth or I will have to face His goodness without any chance of redemption. Any thoughts?

5. Korah gathers _____men and rose up against _____ and _____.

- 16:1-3- The people were really grumbling against the _____.

- 16:11- What happened to Korah's family and his followers? 16:29-35

- What was this fight really about? 17:1-5, 10, Hebrews 5:4

- All would know whom God had chosen because his staff would _____ and grow almonds. 17:5, 8.

7. The priests were _____ by God for service before God in the tent of _____ or tabernacle and the priesthood was a _____. 17:6-7

- Would the sons of Aaron get some land when they get in the Promised Land? 17:20. Did this mean that the LORD would not take care of them? 17:20

Read Chapter 22. There is a talking donkey. You know you are curious.

- Balaam is a prophet and <u>Balak</u> asks him to _____ the nation of Israel. 22:1-6. God speaks to Balaam and says you will not curse them for they are _____ 22:7-12

- God tests Balaam but he follows the princes of _____. 22:21.

- Balaam wanted to please _____ more than God and so God used a _____ to speak to him. 22:22-31.

- In 22:9, God asked Balaam, "Who are these men with you?"
  ➢ After reading the story does it seem like God was confusing Balaam? Remember that God knows all things, including the evil or righteous deeds of a man's heart. Also, in verse 8, Balaam allowed these men to lodge with him. The word "lodge" in Hebrew means to stay or abide. They were staying there in order to convince him to curse Israel and he was okay with that. You have further evidence when you look at Deuteronomy 23:5, Joshua 13:22, Micah 6:5, 2 Peter 2:15, Jude verse 11. Always let scripture interpret scripture so you can find God's truth.

  ➢ What was Balaam's real motive in this narrative (story)? 2 Peter 2:15

8. In Numbers 25:3, Israel yoked (joined as one) himself to the _____ of Peor. They were worshipping other gods.

- Whenever they yoked themselves with other nations, they began to worship other gods. There is only _____ God and he will not allow his people to do so. Read Deuteronomy 4:35, Exodus 20:3.

- While they were weeping over the deaths of those that worshipped Baal, an Israelite man brings a Midianite (another nation) woman into the camp and has sex with her. So when Phinehas the priest saw this, he went and stabbed them once and they both died.

- Phineas acted with zeal and righteousness, so the LORD's _____ did not consume them all. 25:10-11

  ➢ After reading these last two biblical stories about real men and women, you may be beginning to have a different view of the Bible. Many think that the Bible is just about a bunch of do's and dont's and while this is part of it, there is so much more than that. It is primarily about the heart of God and drawing mankind to desire in their hearts to serve and love Him in all things. Thus, the do's and dont's become about obedience and a joy to serve their King, the King of the universe. You are constantly learning about God's character and His intense love for His people. Guess what, if you are a believer, you are one of His people. You have many of the same laws to live under and many of the same blessings to receive. Will you obey or walk in the spirit of Balaam, who was prideful and loved fame and money more than man?

A. Memory Verse: Numbers 23:19 (Write it out here).

B. Six questions to ask while thinking back through the text.

1. Who were the righteous men in the book of Numbers?

2. What does God think of worshipping other gods and questioning those in authority?

3. When could the people have entered into the Promised Land?

4. Where were they supposed to go ever since they left Egypt?

5. Why is it important to only worship God? Deut. 4:35, Isa. 44.8-17

6. How could they have entered the promised land?

C.Application
How does this biblical truth affect how I live my life each day?

D.Journal and prayer time. Is there a sin you need to confess? Will you have faith like Joshua and Caleb? Praise God for helping you in this area of your life.

Lesson 12: Are We There Yet? (Book of Deuteronomy)

Have you ever taken a trip with your family or some people you did not really like very much? Well after a long trip with your family, you may have wondered if you liked them very much. Did it seem like whatever could go wrong did so? Well, this is almost 40 years later and the Israelites are still not in Canaan (Promised Land). What has not gone wrong? They have had many chances to obey, but when you have that many people who are supposed to get along, anything and everything can go wrong. Do you want to see if they make it this time? This lesson is over the entire book of Deuteronomy. Read as much as you can. It is a more of a narrative and thus reads easier than Leviticus, so read as much as you can.

As you begin, remember that Deuteronomy is primarily a retelling of things that God has taught through Moses, but still new truths are revealed. These are Moses' last words to a new generation, so they are extremely important even for us today. Another important point to remember about Deuteronomy is written as a legal document, specifically a Suzerainty Treaty between a king and his vassals, and in this case the King of the Universe and those that are part of His kingdom. This is covenantal language as we have discussed before.

1. Moses is up in age and these are his last words to the people before they go in to the Promised Land. God will not allow Moses to go in, but he still cares for the people.

   • What part of the covenant has been fulfilled in 1:10? Gen. 15:5.

   • What command and promise does he give that they have heard before? 1:8, 11, Genesis 17:8, 28:4, 48:4, Exodus 19:5, Leviticus 14:34, Numbers 13:30, 33:53

   • By looking at all these verses, you know that God wants to keep His _____,

     but the people need to _____. Deuteronomy (Deut.) 1:32.

   • From Egypt to Canaan was less than 250 miles. So what should have taken days has turned into over 38 years and it will be 40 years by the time they are finished with this part of the journey.

     ➢ How is this practical for you today?

2. What happened to the previous generation?   2:14

- Who had prevented them from going into Canaan?   2:15   Whose actions brought this about?

- This is a _____generation, so they need to prove they will obey.

- _____will begin to make a way for the people to enter the land? 2:25

3. There is a phrase, "_____ to _____" that you see in 2:34, 3:6 and will see numerous times in the future. This means that they were to leave no

_____. 2:34.

> The word "cherem" means devote to destruction or to devote to holiness. Again, this is one of those concepts that some of you may struggle with unless you have some explanation. Remember God knows people's hearts and the future (9:4). He knows that if they leave survivors, then His people will begin to worship their gods, disobey Him and live as evil people. He is trying to protect them from the consequences that are sure to follow. On the other hand, if you devote yourself to God and His ways, it will transform your life for the good. Yeshua repeats this concept in Matthew 6:24.

❖ **Definitive Idea: Learning**- There are primarily 2 ways to learn things—You can learn the easy way by learning from other people's mistakes or you can learn the hard way by making your own mistakes and suffering the consequences. Of course these mistakes are often called sins and you must repent and come back to God's laws, His loving boundaries. My advice: Learn some things from your parents and other wiser men and women so you can avoid some serious consequences that may ruin your life! I would like to tell you that I have not seen men and women make these decisions and end up in prison, destroying families, etc., but I would be lying. It really happens.

4. Read Deut. 4:7-8, 35-40.

- Moses reminds the people to obey the statutes of God.

- What does God teach the new generation in Deuteronomy 5?

5. Deuteronomy 6:4-9 is a passage that I have memorized. It is your memory verses for this lesson. I know it is longer than what you have been doing, but these are key verses in scripture, for several reasons. First, these are great instructions for parenting and passing on a Godly heritage. Next, these words are confirming covenant every time you say them. You are declaring who God is, what He has done and how you will live before Him; Covenant language.

- In Hebrew, this passage is called the Shema (to hear and obey).

    - **Illustration**: I have 3 children and when I tell them to do something, I do not want them to just hear me, but to obey me. I do not give instructions to hear myself talk and I love them enough to give them instructions that will guide and protect them in life. If I care this much about my children, how much more does the Creator, the Father of all people, love His children?

6. Why did God choose the nation of Israel? Was it bias or racism as some say? Deut. 7:7-8, Romans 9:4-5

- God chose the nation of Israel because they were the greatest nation. T or F

- God chose them because He loves them and is a covenant keeper. T or F

- God chose them and with this, gave them the responsibility to bring truth and be a light in a sinful, dark world. T or F

7. In Deuteronomy 10:16, Moses points back to _____ which was the sign of the covenant in Genesis 17:10. Circumcision was a _____ act that showed what was happening spiritually in one's _____. 10:16.

8. Read Deuteronomy 13:1-5 and 18:15-22 now. You can see the difference between a _____ prophet and a _____ prophet. Read Mark 12:14, 13:22. Jesus was also a prophet.

- A true prophet can be wrong sometimes? T   or   F

- A true prophet will obey the teachings of God (Torah) and fear the LORD. T or F

    ➢ Just because someone says they are a prophet of God does not mean they are. Satan is actively working to deceive many people. The more you study God's Word, the more you will know truth. Pray for a daily desire to love Him more than the world.

9. Read Deuteronomy 24:5.

❖ **Definitive Idea**: **Marriage**- You learned a little about relationships when you studied about Isaac and Rebekah and the difference between marriage God's way and the world's way. "When a man gets married........he shall be free at home one year to be happy with his wife whom he has taken." Deut. 24:5. I have given this advice to many young people that were engaged or courting. I know not all of you are about to get married, but most of you will one day. I am talking to the guys on this next part, but ladies, you should read it to because you will marry a guy (obviously).

I know that if you told your parents you wanted to live with them at their house for a year they would probably think you were being lazy or just crazy. However, it could be an adjoining garage apartment or maybe some construction could be done so you could stay there, in order to keep expenses and responsibility down some that first year in order to focus on the covenant that you have just made.

I fully realize that in our culture, this seems a bit abnormal, but I have said for years that we need to do Bible things in Bible ways, despite our cultural expectations. After all, believers should desire to obey God's best ways so that we may experience His best everyday. Nevertheless, some family conditions may not work and if you do not follow after Deuteronomy 24, that is still okay. Furthermore, within our current culture this is not easy because no one plans for this and we are so far removed from a covenant idea of marriage that you will probably do it like most couples.

With this said, you can still make different choices that first year. After all, the first year of marriage is the toughest in most cases. If you just take a week off for spring break or vacation, get married and then return to life as if nothing happened, I think you are missing the idea of the covenant you have just entered into under God. Marriage is for life so start off the right way! Here are some practical ideas to begin your covenant:

✓ Pray often for your spouse or future spouse that he/she will walk in the will of God.

✓ Pray for yourself that you will put his/her needs in front of yours.

✓ Take fewer classes if you are in school. Speed of graduation is not the goal.

✓ Only work the hours you need to work (material possessions are temporary, but a covenant is for life).

✓ Don't plan extracurricular activities just for yourself, but plan some things you can do together to see what you like.

✓ Do projects together at home like painting, planting a garden, etc.

✓ Lastly, when you get upset with your spouse, before you say something to him/her, ask yourself what you may have done to start what is happening in your home? This will sometimes end the problem before it begins. I could say more but that is part of my series where I teach this in much more detail.

10. In Deuteronomy chapters 28-29, God says that you will receive _____ for obedience and curses for _____.

11. Read Deut. 29:1-16 and in vs. 14-15 God renews His covenant by saying "It is not with you _____that I am making this covenant, but with _____is standing here."

- This covenant is for all nations, as long as they _____.

   To be part of God's covenant today, a person still has something to do. I talked to you several lessons ago about the fact that a person with salvation will walk in grace, faith, repentance and obedience. Without any of these, it is not what the bible calls a journey of salvation.

   ➤ I want you to look at 2 verses—one you may have heard of and one you may not have, but look and see if they give the same message. Deut. 30:11-20 and John 3:16-21. When you hear the truth of salvation (gospel) you can choose life or death? <u>What have you chosen?</u>

12. Who will take over leadership after Moses dies? 31:1-8

- He gives him some great advice, "Be strong and _____. Do not _____ them, for it is the LORD your God who goes with you. He will not leave you or _____ you. 31:6-8

13. Does Moses get to enter the Promised Land? Why or Why not? Deut. 34:4, 1:22, 37, Exodus 32:19, Numbers 20:12.

- There are two issues that kept Moses out of Canaan, but one blinded him to other issues and thus did not lead the people to God as he should have.

- In Numbers 20:9-12, you get the biggest reason why. The people grumbled again and God told Moses, "You shall bring out water from the rock by speaking to the rock _____their eyes. Instead, Moses _____ the rock and "you did not uphold me as _____ in the eyes of the people of Israel."

- Moses let his anger get the best of him and it led to a scene that was prideful and without patience, thus instead of bringing glory to the LORD, it was about Moses.

  ➢ What does this tell you about those that lead others for God? Moses was meeker than any other man on the earth, but he had an anger problem at times. No leader will be perfect, but honor them as they walk in righteousness. Pray, encourage and hold them accountable to speak the truth and live out God's Word.

.**A. Memory Verse**: Write out Deuteronomy 6:4-6, (you can learn verses 7-9 if you would like). I would love for some of you to learn all six verses as I have. It is a powerful passage of Scripture. Go to my website www.only1way.net and share how these verses have changed you and your family. I would love to share my testimony with you too.

B. Six questions to ask while thinking back through the text.

1. Who was meeker than any other man?

2. What happens when you walk in obedience?

3. When will you not be blessed?

4. Where is God looking to see what kind of young man/woman you are?

5. Why did Moses not enter the Promised Land?

6. How is marriage a covenant? Do some research and know that it involves blood, physically, if done God's way and it is for life. Is it based on emotions or on a daily commitment to love each other?

C. <u>Application</u>

How does this biblical truth affect how I live my life each day?

D. Journal and prayer time. Is there a sin you need to confess? As you do this, ask God to help you live according to what you have just studied. Praise God for caring so much about you.

Lesson 13: Let the Battles Begin (Joshua)

I told you much earlier that salvation was a journey. Are you starting to believe that? It is not like our world where we want everything fast—food, Internet, texting, packages, movies, etc. Your salvation is about a lifetime of growth, so make the most of everyday. Slow down enough to take the focus off of yourself and onto others. Love people, rest and enjoy life as you live daily to bring God glory. Speaking of fast, let's get to the lesson. See, I get in a hurry as well.

Moses has died and Joshua is the new leader to lead them from this point on. Will they actually get in this time? Will they finally obey consistently? You need to read Joshua. As I have said before, I do not know if you are reading all that I suggest, but do your best and be honest with God about your efforts. Joshua has some very interesting things including war. Have you realized by now that there are parts of the Bible that would be rated "R" for violence, sexual content, and evil? There is war because they don't get in without a fight. Your salvation is a battle (many things that are physical are connected to the spiritual parts of your life). Are you armed? Look at Ephesians 6:10-18 before you start concerning the preparation for battle. Winning battles for God each day involves the spiritual first.

1. Was the land theirs for the taking? Why? Joshua 1:2-3, Deuteronomy 1:21

2. What three things does the LORD tell Joshua that he must do to have success? 1:6-8

    • Do the first two depend upon obedience to the third one?
    • What phrase is repeated 3 times in these verses?

3. How did the people respond to the words of Joshua? Compare to Exodus 19:8.

4. Joshua sends in the spies and they take refuge in the house of Rahab, a prostitute.
    • What did she tell the messengers of the King? 2:4

    • _____ "lied" to protect the righteous from the unrighteous. 2:3-5. As discussed before, God honors the lives of the righteous. Hebrews 11:31, James 2:25.
    • Due to the reputation of the God of Israel, there is great _____ among the people and leaders in the land. 2:8-12

5. What was the sign that would save Rahab? Do you remember what type of covenant a person enters into when saved?

   - Though your sins are like _____, they shall be white as snow. Isaiah 1:18
   - Each generation was looking for the Messiah and each generation was getting closer. Read Matthew 1:5 to see that _____ is included in the line leading to the Messiah?

6. The sign for the people to cross the Jordan River and take the land is the _____ of the covenant. 3:3

   - The Ark of the Covenant represented the dwelling place of _____. Exodus 25:8. It was located in the Most _____ Place inside the tabernacle. Hebrews 9:3, Exodus 25:8-22

   - What was in the Ark of the Covenant? Hebrews 9:4

   - They had the full tabernacle that contained the Ark of the Covenant and now they are just bringing the Ark of the Covenant for their entrance into the land.

7. Read Joshua 3:10-17 and look at the covenant of God (His promises) continuing.
   - Look back to Genesis 15:17-21 and Exodus 14:21-25 to see the promises and the cycles. As you continue to study the Holy Scriptures, you will see that God works in cycles, and is so consistent and true. Trust and obey God who is always be the same. There is so much hope and comfort in this truth.

8. What happens in 5:2-3 and why? Genesis 17:9-10. It was a _____ of the covenant between God and his people. Was this required of the men as part of the covenant?

9. In obedience to Leviticus 23:4, they celebrated the _____ in Joshua 5:10.

10. Read Joshua 6. It is a great event in of God's redemptive history of our world. The priests are to take up the Ark of the Covenant and the people of Israel are commanded to march around the city for _____days. Then the priests would blow the _____ and the people were to give a great _____. The walls to the city _____ down flat and they were told to devote to _____.

➢ As you are reading this, do you have any questions or would you have done things different than God? I have also thought about some of these things. This teaches you that God's ways can be questioned, but ultimately you must obey. If they had only marched around 6 days, skipped day 7 and then started again on day 8, would God have blessed them in this battle? Why or why not?

11. What caused Israel to be defeated in chapter 7:1-12?

• God cannot be with sinful people so every sin severs your relationship with God. When you are living in sin, do not expect God to answer your prayers or to bless your life. Don't confuse a blessed or prosperous life with attaining material possessions. You prosper as your soul prospers in the Lord.

• There is a difference between living in a sinful state of imperfection and living in intentional sin. One is because of circumstances that started with Adam and Eve and one is your own sinful desire. James 1:13-15.

• The people devote their own to _____ by eliminating the sin from within their midst. After this, the defeat of Ai came easy.

12. All the kings of the land _____ together to fight against Joshua and Israel. 9:1-2

13. The Gibeonites feared the Israelites, so they deceive Joshua into making a _____

with them. Joshua did not ask for _____ from the LORD. 9:14

• Nothing is too big or little to seek the counsel of the LORD before making a decision. Some of you think you have all the answers while some of you only listen to your group of friends. Take a higher road and seek the truth of God at all times. He created you so Father knows best. Your heavenly Father loves (is loyal or committed) to you always.

14. What cool event happens in Joshua 10:12-15?

➢ This would be called a miracle because if this actually happened, it would bring chaos to our world. If you love science or if you want to see God's amazing fingerprints on creation, buy the DVD Privileged Planet. God created the sun in Genesis 1:16, and since he created it He can change how it works if he wants to. God is awesome in power.

15. Joshua is told to _____the land for an inheritance to the _____ tribes and half

tribe of Manasseh. 13:7.

- How many tribes were left out and what about their inheritance? 1:12-13, 13:8, Numbers 32:33-41

- Concerning the _____, the _____ is their inheritance. 13:14, Numbers 18:20.

16. How were the Israelites disobedient to God as they were taking over the land of the covenant? Deut. 20:16-18, 31:16, Joshua 13:13, 15:63, 16:10.

- Did God keep His covenant despite their disobedience? 21:45

➢ Will they receive the same blessings in the land because they disobeyed than if they had obeyed? Why or why not?

17. Now that they disobeyed, God has to remind them about something, "that you may not

_____with these nations remaining with you." Exodus 23:13, Joshua 23:7.

- Remember the Tree of the Knowledge of Good and Evil from Genesis 2-3.
- This command not to mix includes no _____ to them. 23:12
- You cannot be married to someone and not be influenced by them in some ways, which is why the Apostle Paul says, "_____from sexual immorality for every other _____ a person commits is outside the body, but the sexually immoral person sins against his own body." **2 Corinthians 6:14-18.**
- In vs. 13 the Bible says what will happen if you mix: "know for certain that the LORD your God will no longer drive out these nations before you, but they shall be a _____ and a _____ for you."

❖ **Definitive Idea: <u>Sex and our culture</u>**- I know you get a lot of mixed messages when it comes to sex. The world says it is okay, it makes you an adult, and it is your business. Then your pastor and parents are saying that it is wrong until marriage and you should stay sexually pure. Ultimately it comes down to "Who should I listen to on this matter"? The answer is found in 1 John 3:3 and other scriptures. "And everyone who thus hopes in him _____ himself as He is _____. (also see Psalm 119:9). See God is pure which is why it is right to stay pure until marriage. God does not decide to be pure, but is pure 100% of the time, no exceptions; not to mention He created you. Read 1 John 3:1-2 now. Therefore, you are his child and as a child of God, you have entered into a blood covenant with a Holy and pure God. There are laws to obey in this covenant and you obey your heavenly Father just as you obey your earthly Father: out of love and joy in response for all He has done for you. <u>You do this not because someone else tells you to or because you have decided to do it, but because the God of the universe created sex as pure because His character is pure.</u> His boundaries are given to you out of love. If you are still not convinced to do it God's way, look up statistics of STD's, AIDS, infertility due to STD's, children born out of wedlock and adultery, just to name a few. Any sins that you need to confess and repent before God so you may be healed, James 5:16?

▪ **Illustration**: A fireplace is a great place to have a fire in the winter. It is nice to look at and is warm and safe. However, if you take those logs out of the fireplace and light them in the middle of the living room, it will destroy your whole house. There is a great and safe place to have a fire in your house. Just like marriage is the safe place to have sex in life and having sex outside of marriage can and often will destroy your life.

18. Read chapter 24 at this time because it is a great summary of what has happened from Abram until now in your history.
19. The people have a choice to make and Joshua sets the example by saying, "As for me and my _____, we will _____ the LORD. 24:15.

• What are the 3 reasons given that they should choose God in 24:13?

- Who do the people choose?

- What do they have to do first in order to be right with God? 24:23

A. **Memory Verse:** Joshua 1:16, write it out here.

B. **Six questions to ask while thinking back through the text.**

1. Who finally brings the people into the Promised Land?

2. What kind of man was Joshua?

3. When should they have entered the Promised Land?

4. Where do they cross and was this similar to a previous point in history involving water?

5. Why were they defeated by the small nation of Ai?

6. How did they get restored back to the LORD?

C. **Application**

How does this biblical truth affect how I live my life each day?

D. **Journal and prayer time**. Is there a sin you need to confess? As you do this, ask God to help you live according to what you have just studied. Praise God for his continued faith in your life even when you are faithless.

Lesson 14: Evil Abounds (Judges and Beginning of 1 Samuel)

If you would like to get a small summary of what has happened thus far in God's redemptive history, then read Psalms 105 and 106. If you are really in a mood to read some great history, then read Judges. These are some of my favorite and intriguing stories of real men in your history, so I encourage you to read them. As I am sure you have noticed, there are several verses that you are reading in different parts of the Bible. I am not doing this just so you can learn your Bible better, although that is good, but I am doing it so you will see the consistency, the connections, and the absolute truth of the Word of God. If you do this each week yet doubt the Word of God, then you doubt Him. It is okay to have some sincere doubts and struggles while learning about God, but there must come a day when your faith rules over your doubts, so when God speaks, you quickly want to obey. It took me several years as a believer to get to this point where I believe every word of God's Word. I did not say I know it all yet or obey it all perfectly, but I did say that I believe it all. God is truth and so I believe it all. With this said, be sure to read as many of the other verses as possible as you continue in this journey of faith. Are you ready to see what happens next? Are you noticing that you could easily make a great and exciting movie from the pages of the Bible that you have studied up to this point? Who knows; maybe you will be the next great producer that will do this to honor God.

1. _____took over for Joshua after he died. Judges 1:2.

2. What phrase do you see again 6 times from Judges 1:21-33?

3. God responds by saying, "I will not drive them out before you, but they shall become

    _____in your side and their _____shall be a snare to you. 2:3

4. What phrase begins to appear in 3:12, 4:1, 6:1?

   • Do you think this behavior will get them the blessing of the land?

5. What was a curse (Deut. 28) or consequence of disobedience found in 6:1-2?

   • It was the LORD's fault that they were under Midian rule for 7 years. T or F

   • _____is a righteous man that destroys the altar of _____ to help

      restore the nation of Israel. 6:28-32.

   • Gideon uses only _____men to defeat the _____.

      This happened so _____would get the glory. 7:2-3

      ➤ Does God need an army or can he do it by himself? Why do you think he asks you and
         me to do many things for Him in our lifetime? How will it help you to do God's will?
         Ephesians 2:10, Matthew 5:16

6. _____acts like many politicians and movie stars. It is all about what is best for him. 9:1-3.

- Did Abimelech have God's favor like Gibeon did? 9:22-23
- Abimelech died by getting hit over the head by a _____. 9:53
- Who threw the rock? _____ And you thought the idea of a man being embarrassed for being shown up by a woman is new? Some things never change. 9:53

7. What phrase is still seen in 13:1?

8. There was a certain man of Zorah of the Danites whose name was _____ and his wife was _____ (could not have children). An angel of the LORD appeared to his wife and said, "You shall conceive a _____. He shall be a _____ and shall begin to save Israel from the Philistines. 13:1-5.

- A Nazirite (to be set apart) could not shave his head or cut his hair, could not touch anything unclean, nor could he drink wine or strong drink. Numbers 6
- _____is born and when he grows up, he seeks to marry a _____woman. 14:1-3

9. Read Judges 14-16 now. Yes you really want to! In 14:3, Samson says, "Get her for me, for she is right in _____ own eyes.

- Was it about Samson or should it have been about what is right to God?
- Was it part of God's plan to defeat the Philistines? 14:4

10. Samson puts forth a riddle for the Philistines and they cannot figure it out for 3 days, so they want Samson's wife to find out the answer.

- His wife uses _____to get him to answer. For the guys- When a girl or woman tries to use this to get her way, know that this has been used for centuries. I say no more. Joshua 14:16
- His wife continues by saying, "You only hate me; you do not love me. You have put a riddle for _____ _____. 14:16. Samson should not have married her because blood is thicker than water. Read what God said would happen in Deuteronomy 31:16.

11. God is still with Samson at this point and he escapes from the Philistines that want to harm him. 15:1-16.

12. How long did Samson rule as judge in Israel? 15:20 _____.

13. In 16:1, Samson pursues another wife named _____. Did he not learn anything the first time?

- The lords of the _____ told her to _____ him and find out why he is so _____. 16:4-5

- What are the 3 ways he says are the secret to removing his strength in 16:7-14?

14. Delilah pulls out another secret weapon and says, "How can you say I _____ you when your heart is not with me? She is playing unfair. Does it work? What was the real secret to his strength? 16:17

- What does Samson do in verse 28 that is so important to our lives even today?

- Does God answer his repentant cry for help?

15. When did the fall of Samson really begin?

➢ The story of Samson brings us to possibly question God. God planned to free His people from under Philistine rule, but it seems to appear that He chooses the method of intermarriage to accomplish this. As I said before, it is okay to question God, but do this in humility and seeking after truth, not in arrogance. God knows the heart of man and the intermarriage did prove fatal for Samson, but he repented and was able to carry out God's plan. Did God know Samson would marry these women anyway? Did God know what test it would take for Samson to have a humble, repentant heart?

BOOK OF 1 SAMUEL

16. As you open the book of 1Samuel, you will see a woman named _____ who is barren. She cries out (prays) to God and says that if God will give her a _____ , she will dedicate him as a Nazirite.

17. The LORD raises up a prophet and judge named _____ to replace _____ the current prophet. 1 Samuel 2:27, 2-35, and chapter 3.

18. God rejected Eli because of the _____ (Genesis 6:5) and worthlessness of his sons, _____ and _____ . 2:12, 34.

19. For this same reason, you see Israel lose _____ men in battle to the Philistines.

- They decide that the solution to victory is to take the Ark of the Covenant with them and this time Israel loses 30,000 men and the _____ . 4:1-11.

- Do you remember what the Ark represented?

- What happened in 4:11 that was the real solution to achieving victory? They were to purge (remove) the _____ from among them. Deut. 17:8-13.

- Who actually purged the evil? 2:34

20. Is there anyone that can stand against the one true God?

- Even the Philistine false god, _____ falls on his face before the Ark of the LORD. After they saw the false god laying on his face, they picked it back up and the second day, it was on its face again and now its _____ and _____ were cut off and laying on the floor. 5:1-5

- The Philistines were then inflicted with _____ and _____ , so they sent the Ark back to Israel. 5:6, 6:4-5.

21. Israel _____and puts away their Baals and Ashtaroth, and served the _____ only. 7:3-4, (Numbers 5:5-8 for repentance in lesson 11 #1).

22. The people want a king to be _____every other nation. 1 Samuel 8:1-6.

➤ **Critical Thought**: **Popularity or Tolerance**- Many of you are at a time in your life where you are selfish and yet insecure. You want to be independent but yet liked by everyone. You are not like everyone else, but are to be holy (set apart). Read Leviticus 19:1-2. Many people will tell you that you are free to make your own choices. While it is true that you have freedom in Christ, the freedom is to be obedient and thus not be chained to the consequences of your bad decisions. Some will tell you it is okay to just get along with everyone and blend in, but the Bible clearly states that you are to be different, set apart for a purpose by your loving Creator.

Have fun, but make sure that the fun fits in to the freedom that you have in Jesus the Christ. God did not save His people out of bondage from Egypt to go back into bondage by thinking freedom meant you can do whatever you want to do. Instead He gave them His laws to live by. Why would God take you from bondage to sin to bondage of "freedom?" If you understand God's instructions, you understand true freedom! At some point, you will have to choose a side in life! Luke 16:13

▪ **Definitive idea**: **Making Decisions**- You are watching a movie by yourself and you realize that it has a few more bad words than you thought it would. It bothers you but you think that it would probably be okay to sit through it. After all, the plot seems pretty good and you really like Nicolas Cage movies (or whoever your favorite actor or actress is). It is not for me to decide if you should get up and leave, and there is not simply "a right or wrong answer" to this. I can give you some thoughts on how you make come to a decision on this. First of all, what is your motivation to do all things? To bring glory to God would be the answer. We could look at this scenario and say that they are not using the real serious curse words except once and they are not using the names Jesus or God, so it is probably okay. You need to ask yourself some questions:

1. Can I watch this and be unaffected in my walk with God?
2. Am I really feeling okay about it or am I trying to justify it?
3. Does the language just kind of blend in and thus no big deal?
4. Is it that big of a deal to watch this, as I do not watch that many movies?
5. Would I watch it if I was with people that I respected in the LORD?
6. Would I watch it with my parents around?
7. Does it draw me closer to God or further away?
8. Can I watch this through a biblical lens, thus keeping my mind engaged, and enjoy it but stay keenly aware of the worldview that they may be trying to teach me?

This really comes down to your maturity level, your wisdom, and the motives and desires of your heart. Can you handle this? What are the motives and desires for your actions this week? Do you really need to watch it? In other words, are there no other movies you could watch or could you just do something else? Decisions are not the same for every believer in every situation but handling something in maturity does not necessarily mean you need to do it. Pray and obey God. Any movie or television programs come to mind? Any thoughts?

23. Samuel lists 7 things that a king will do if they get a king, 8:10-18

- Who were the people rejecting by wanting a king? 8:7

  They already had a king, the _____ of the universe. Psalm 47:7.

- Even with the warning, the people said. "There shall be a king over us." 8:19.

24. In 1 Samuel 10:1, Samuel the prophet _____ Saul with oil and he is appointed by God to be king over the nation of Israel. In 10:9-10, the _____ of God comes upon Saul to guide him to be a great king.

25. In Samuel's farewell speech, he warns them that "if" they will _____ God and _____ Him, it will be okay, but if they do not, then the consequences will be great. 12:6-22

A. Memory Verse- Judges 2:11, Write it out here.

B. **Six questions to ask while thinking back through the text.**

1. Who tried to warn the people and who was the first king of Israel?

2. What tribe did he come from?

3. When did Samson's downfall begin?

4. Where was Samson's strength physically and spiritually?

5. Why didn't Samson just refuse to tell his secret?

6. How could the Philistines have been defeated as opposed to how it happened (choices)?

C. Application

How does this biblical truth affect how I live my life each day?

D. Journal and prayer time. Is there a sin you need to confess? As you do this, ask God to help you live according to what you just studied? Praise Him for small victories over sin.

Lesson 15: King Saul vs. King David (1 and 2 Samuel)

Do you like a good rivalry? What are some good rivalries in the movies? Spiderman and the Green Goblin, Batman and the Joker, Aslan and the white witch of Narnia. I am sure you can think of a few others. The rivalry or battle between good and evil rages on and in this next lesson, you will see how God reacts to his leader that walks in righteousness (good) and his leader that walks in unrighteousness (evil). Have you realized by now that the very same idea that began in Genesis (the beginning), is still the same today? You see this battle between good and evil in everything from cartoons, movies, relationships, business, politics, etc. It is everywhere and it will not change until Jesus the Christ returns and finally defeats Satan, the king of evil.

1. Saul barely begins his reign and he has "not sought the _____ of the LORD." 13:12. Thus "your _____ shall not continue. The LORD has sought a man after his own _____. 13:14, also see Acts 13:22. Samuel was the priest and was supposed to offer the sacrifices according to Exodus and Leviticus.

2. Read 14:24-46 so that you can understand what is happening. Saul makes a _____ and says "cursed be the man who _____ food until it is evening and I have avenged my enemies. His son _____ did not hear him and eats some food. 14:27.

- The basic lesson is to control your tongue and the deeper meaning that will be discussed later is to avoid making vows for yourself or others. Yeshua said let your "yes" be yes and your "no" be no. We do not need to swear by anything. Matthew 5:37

➢ **Extreme Thought: Controlling the Tongue-** I wanted to take a moment here and ask you how much you think about your words, what comes out of your mouth each day? Many young people struggle with this. Since you are at the most selfish time of your life (teenage years and at age 2), you love to speak (I didn't come up with these facts). In fact many young people I have been around love to hear their own voice. I don't say this to be rude, but this has been my experience. I still love young people, but sometimes another perspective needs to be brought into the equation. Do not worry, as some adults, including myself, can also struggle at times.

A believer is to obey James 1:19, "Be quick to listen, slow to speak, and slow to become angry." God gave you 2 ears and only 1 mouth so I think He was telling you to listen twice as much as you talk. Can you write something down here? How would your school and your family change if you obeyed this verse? Do not worry about trying to change others, but focus upon yourself. Get a friend and you both practice this for a week and see what happens. <u>Write it down and I would love to hear how it changed your perspective and your life.</u> *God saved you to change you and we all need change in this area.*

- Saul actually listened to the people and did not kill his own son. As you get to know Jonathon some in this lesson, you will be glad he did not kill him. 14:45.

3. Saul gets another chance to obey God and do what is right (ch. 15). Samuel tells him that he is to attack _____ and devote to _____ 15:2-3. Amalek opposed Israel and if you are not for Israel you are against them. 15:2. If you are against Israel, you are against the holy God of Israel- Genesis 12:3

- In 15:21, what was Saul's explanation of what he had done in order to obey what God had said?

- What specifically did God tell him to do in 15:3?

- Why was it a bad idea to do what Saul did in 15:21?

- Does God ask us for obedience in our wisdom or in His? Deuteronomy 4:6

  ❖ **Wise (wisdom) defined** (*Chokmah* and *Sakal* in Hebrew)- "The ability to consider a situation with comprehension in order to be successful or prosperous." [19] It is applied knowledge of God and His ways; to walk circumspect before God. If you make decisions or decide to do something based upon a lack of knowledge or disobedience to God, you will fail or at least not do it at its best. There is a vast difference between man's wisdom and God's wisdom (1 Corinthians 1:25). For more explanation see Jeremiah 10:12, Romans 11:33, Proverbs 1:7, 9:10. You also see wisdom in the building of the temple in Exodus 31:1-5.

- Did Adam and Eve apply wisdom? They knew good from evil, but chose not to apply _____ and thus sinned.

- In 15:28, Samuel says to Saul, "The LORD has torn the kingdom of _____ from you this day and has given it to a neighbor of yours, who is better than you.

- What did Samuel do to the king of Amelek in 15:33?

  <u>Pretty gruesome stuff, but remember God is continually letting his people know how serious He is about obedience. God knows best and His laws are put in place as loving boundaries and if you disobey, the world of sin will consume you.</u>

4. God chooses a man to be king based upon the condition of his _____ but man looks on the _____ appearance. 16:7

- What kind of man did the nation want? 9:2, 10:23

5. God sent Samuel to the house of Jesse to choose one of his 7 sons to be the next king.

- Who was Jesse and why is this important? Ruth 4:17, Matthew 1:5-6, 16.

- In 16:13, Samuel "anointed _____ and the Spirit of the LORD rushed upon him and the Spirit left _____ and an evil spirit tormented him. Even though the evil spirit was upon him, God sent David to play _____ for him to bring him comfort. God extends grace to Saul.

- David came to Saul and entered his service and Saul _____ him greatly. 16:21

6. In chapter 171-11, the Philistine giant Goliath comes against Israel and _____ and all of _____ was afraid. For _____ days, Goliath came forward and no Israelite would fight him. 17:16.

- In 17:27, David says, "Who is this uncircumcised Philistine, that he should defy the armies of the _____ God?

- Do you remember why being circumcised is so important? Genesis 17

- There are those "in covenant" and those "out of covenant." To be "in covenant" meant that you have a promise from God and could enter into a blood covenant in order to be saved. Someone "in covenant" would strive to obey all of the Torah (laws or teachings of God) because in them you find the character and nature of God for daily living (Exodus 19:5, 23:21, Romans 7:13-8:2). Torah often refers to the first 5 books of the bible, but Torah in a broader sense, is the laws or the teachings of God for his people. Obedience to Torah does not save you, but teaches you how to live when you are saved.

❖ **Torah (Law) Defined** (torah in Hebrew)- a pointing of your finger or an object to show which way to walk or live; to point the way or direction one is to walk in life; teaching, to hit the mark. [20] As you see from this Hebrew definition, the law was really about the right way to go in life, which is God's teachings and commands. If you ever wonder which way you should go, just study and ask (pray) because He cares enough to show you.

- You just learned what Torah means. A common interpretation in your English Bible will be the word "law." This is not a good definition unless you have more explanation. I have given you some already, but I want to give you this illustration to help you more.

- **Illustration:** You are at home in the kitchen. You reach for something that is a little tough to reach and while doing this with one hand; your other hand accidentally falls into the boiling water that your mom was using to make some hot tea. The law of God says that at 212 degrees Fahrenheit, water boils and your skin is not made to deal with this temperature. Did God punish you by His natural law for your action? Of course not. However there are consequences for your actions. The natural laws of God in the physical world are no different than the ones in the spiritual world. You receive a natural consequence when you break a natural law. When you break a law from a God that sets all laws as holy and righteous, then your breaking of His law will result in missing the mark of holiness and righteousness. Thus there are always consequences to breaking a physical or spiritual law of God. God is not sitting around waiting to condemn you for your sins, but your sins put you in opposition to His perfect ways, His laws. If you make up your own laws, you automatically defy God's laws. God's laws protect and govern our lives. Obeying God's laws do not save you for eternity, but reveal your heart, your desire and continual bearing of good fruit. Ephesians 2:8-10

7. Why are there still Philistines to defy God's people? Judges 3:1-5

- David is ready but Saul says, "You are not able to go against this Philistine to fight with him, for you are but a _____. 17:33, 1 Timothy 4:12.

  ➤ Do you think God only uses old people or he only uses young people? He uses all who are obedient and willing to fight for what is right.

- In 17:45, David says that Goliath comes with weapons, but David comes in the _____ of the LORD of _____, the God of the armies of Israel. David only uses one _____ to kill the giant.

8. David and Jonathan, Saul's _____ become best friends and loved one another.

   ❖ **Definitive Thought: Manhood-** I know that in our current culture with the openness of homosexuality, some may read this and think it seems funny for two guys to love one another. Our culture has painted a picture of men that is not biblical. It is okay for men to be rugged and tough and yet have deep relationships with other men that honor God. Loving another man does not mean you are gay nor does it mean that you are not tough. **Pay Attention Guys**: Let the Bible define you as a man, not the world.

9. How did the women respond to David's battle heroics? 18:7

   • Before going any further, how do you think Saul will react?

   • See Saul's reaction in 18:10-11.

   • Jonathan shows his _____ for David by warning him that Saul was trying to _____ him. 19:1-2 and chapter 20.

   • In 20:15-16, David and Jonathan make a _____. And it says that David loved Jonathan as he loved his own _____. Your soul is your life-spark, it is your whole being, it is that which is knit to God, that which will exist for eternity. David and Jonathan were friends in life and in death.

10. In the remainder of the book of 1 Samuel, you can read about the lives of David and Saul. David spares Saul's life twice (Chapter 24 and 26) because he would not touch the LORD's

_____.

11. In 2 Samuel 2:1-4, David inquires of the _____ and then takes his two wives and goes where God sends him.

   ➢ **Guys: No you cannot have more than one wife at a time so do not have more than one girlfriend at a time**. You will see why in a little bit. If you are not sure, just ask some Godly men and they will tell you it is tough enough to be married to one wife, much less have multiple wives. I don't say this in a negative way, but just to say that marriage takes work and you don't have time to build a solid, lasting relationship with more than one wife.

   • David is anointed King over the house of _____ 2:4. In 5:2-3, David is appointed King over the house of _____.

- There is supposed to only be God's people, altogether as one, but this division of the two houses began in 1 Samuel 11:8.

- "David became greater and greater for the _____ was with him." 5:10. David took more _____ and wives from Jerusalem. You will have to look this word up. Hint: It is not related in any way to porcupines.

  http://www.jewishvirtuallibrary.org/jsource/judaica/ejud_0002_0005_0_04557.html

12. David brings in the Ark of the Covenant on a new _____ and when the ark was about to fall off, _____ reached out to grab it and when touching it, he died. 6:1-7

- What did he do that was so bad? Exodus 25:13-16

- Actually it was not what he did, but it was the disobedience of King _____ because he did not build it according to how God had _____. 6:3, 1 Chronicles 15:12-15.

13. Read 2 Samuel 7. This is an important chapter. David wants to build a _____ for the LORD. The LORD responds by telling David that He will build him a _____.

- The LORD renews the covenant that He had begun with Adam, Noah, Abram, and so on.
- In 7:16, the LOR D says, "And your _____ and your _____ shall be made sure forever before me. Your throne shall be established _____
- The God of the universe, the only true God wants to do all this for David. Was it because David was perfect? Look at Exodus 34:6 to find the answer.

14. David is successful in battle, yet he takes the time in Chapter 9 to remember his covenant with Jonathon, whom he loved like a brother.

- He showed kindness to _____, the son of Jonathan. Some of you may not think this is a big deal, but if you understand how the culture was at that time concerning kings. When a new king took over, no one in the former kings' family was safe. They were considered a threat to take back the throne. David went totally against the culture to do what was right by the covenant.

➢ **Extreme Thought**: What will you do the next time you are faced with a tough moral decision? Will you stand up for what is right even if it is against the culture of your school, your neighborhood, and your peers. You need to write it down and pray about it so that when it comes up, you will do what is right over what is normal or accepted. Preparation is half the battle.

15. David is going along enjoying his great life that God has provided for him and one decision changes his life. David saw a beautiful woman bathing and David sent and _____ about her. 11:1-4. Oh, it gets worse. _____ informs David that she is pregnant. It gets even worse as David tries to get her husband, _____ to sleep with her so he will think the baby is his baby. And when you thought it could not get any worse, David has Uriah placed at the _____ of the heaviest fighting so that he will die. 11:5-24.

- Was David's first sin when he sent for Bathsheba?

- He was king of his army, so where should he have been instead of lounging on the roof? 11:1-2.

- List the sins that he committed against God.

16. Read Chapter 12 and see what happens between Nathan the prophet and King David

- What does David finally do in vs. 13?

- What were David's consequences to his sins? 12:14.

17. There are many more interesting things in David's life. Read as much as you can in chapters 13 through the end of 2 Samuel. You will see how this one event in David's life changed him and thus many consequences followed. He was still saved by God and God still loved him, but his life would have looked so different, if he had obeyed.

➢ **Extreme Thought**: **Obey:** Go back to Lesson 12 #5 for definition - Think right now how much easier your life would be if you would just obey. Are the words "obey" or "obedience" seen in negative or positive terms within the culture? Is this an easy word to take in? Have you noticed that obedience and your salvation are inseparable? To give you a little more clarification, it is important to remember that obeying or serving God is not about guilt or obligation, but about faith, love and joy. Write down an area where you struggle to obey. What changes can you make in this as well as how you perceive the word "obey?"

A. Memory Verse- 2 Samuel 7:22, Write it out.

B. Six questions to ask while thinking back through the text.

1. Who confronted David about his sins?

2. What have you done or seen others do that really changed their lives? It can be painful, right?

3. When does David begin his downward spiral?

4. Where should David have been instead of on the roof?

5. Why does David's sins take him this far? James 1:13-15

6. How did God refer to David despite some sins that he committed? See Acts 13:22. How does this make you feel and how does this help you to grasp how God's grace, love and justice work in harmony?

121

C. Application How does this biblical truth affect how I live my life each day?

D. Journal and prayer time. Is there a sin you need to confess? As you do this, ask God to help you live according to what you just studied. Praise God for His protection and grace, because without it we would be in bad shape.

Lesson 16: Nation of God is Divided/Prophets Arise (1 and 2 Kings)

You are now entering the time when Solomon will build God a permanent dwelling place and the people of God will not move from place to place. Of course, God is not confined to a physical place, but He chose to meet with His people in this manner. Their home will be called the City of David, Zion or Jerusalem. This is the same Jerusalem that you read about today, but they owned much more land at that time and will own more land when the Messiah returns. You are going to be introduced to many prophets during this section. The prophets were often the "spiritual advisors" to the king if they would listen. The Hebrew word means seer or prophet, which describes one who speaks for God out of the truth that God shows him through dreams and visions or God places inside of him. Some of them would speak of what was to come in the future, or what is often called "to speak prophetically," but this term can just mean speaking the truth. Being a prophet was tough because you usually brought a message of truth, but many did not want to hear it. There are many prophets for God still today, but for those who would call themselves prophets, it is defined as those who boldly speak forth the truth of God, and not necessarily speaking about specific events in the future. Prophet is a term that some believe does not exist today and some have abused the term, so for now it is important to understand that most prophets of today are simply speaking forth the truth according to the Word of God. The first time the word "prophet" is used is for Abraham in Genesis 20:7. So prophets are not new to the Bible at this point, but you will begin to read much more about them in this section. Refer back to Lesson 12, #9 for some details.

1. You left off with King David and the consequences of his sins. In 1 Kings you see that David is old and it is time for him to pass his kingship to his son Solomon.

- Would this be an easy task? 1 Kings 1:5-8

- What did Adonijah do wrong in 1:9-10?

- Who was supposed to be king? 2 Samuel 12:24, 1 Kings 1:13
- Solomon is crowned king by the anointing of the _____ and the declaration by _____ the prophet and the blowing of the trumpet. 1:34.

2. David gives Solomon his final instructions. "Keep the charge of the LORD your God, walking in his _____ and keeping his _____, his commandments, his rules and his testimonies as it is written in the _____ of Moses, that you may prosper in all that you do and wherever you turn. 2:1-3. He reminds him in vs. 4 of God's promise to continue the legacy that will eventually lead to the Messiah. 2:45.

3. Solomon acknowledges that God _____ his father David. David obeyed Deuteronomy 6:4-6 and taught him as a father should teach his children. Do you still remember this memory verse? If not, practice it again. It is an extremely important covenant verse.

- Of all the things that Solomon could have chosen, what did he ask God to give him?

  ➢ Think about what you would ask if God would grant you whatever you wanted. Would you ask something that would honor God or yourself?

- Solomon asks for wisdom. Read Proverbs 9:10. If you do not fear the LORD, don't even bother to ask for wisdom. Go back to lesson 15 #3 on wisdom.
- By asking for wisdom, which was to honor God, God also gives him both _____ and _____. 3:13. Read chapter 4 to learn about his wisdom and wealth.

4. It is time for Solomon to build the _____ and the time is right because the LORD has given him _____ on every side. 5:1-4.

- In 5:13-18, how many men did it take to build the temple of the LORD?

- Were there any specific instructions from God? Chapter 6

- What is the "if" statement you see in 6:12? This is the same statement you have seen all the way back to Genesis. God is asking for obedience from his people.

- How long did it take for Solomon to build the house of God and how long to build his own house? 6:38-7:1

- Do you see a possible problem with this?

- In Chapter 8, you will read that it was time to bring in the _____of the covenant and place it in the Most _____Place, underneath the wings of the cherubim (angels). Do you remember what the Ark of the Covenant represented?

5. Solomon recognizes the_____that was made before him and continues now with him. He also understands the God he serves. 8:9, 21-25, 2 Samuel 7:14-16, Exodus 34:6.

- In Chapter 8, Solomon prays in a way that tells you that he knows he needs God. He even says in 8:46, "for there is no one who does not _____." Romans 3:10-23.

- The LORD tells Solomon the same thing he has told every generation up to this point, and that is the fact that you will be blessed for obedience and cursed for disobedience.

6. Just like David, Solomon also was led astray by women. He had_____ wives and _____ concubines and they turned away his heart. 11:1-4. The LORD says in 11:11, you have not kept my _____ and my statutes.

- How many commands did Solomon break from Deuteronomy 17:16-17? _____
- In 11:13-31, God will take the_____ away from Solomon and gives it to an Ephraimite named Jeroboam. He will get _____ tribes.
- For the sake of his servant David, he will still preserve _____ tribes. 11:13, 32.
- In Chapter 12, Rehoboam, Solomon's son takes over the House of Judah and listens to the counsel of the older men.   T or F
- In 12:25-33, Jeroboam sets up high places to worship because he was afraid that if the people went to worship in the temple of _____ as they were supposed to, then he would lose his kingdom. He set them in _____and _____.
- What five laws did he break in 1 Kings 12:28-33?

7. The fifth law he broke has to do with changing God's appointed times. If you have forgotten the definition of this, go back to Lesson 10 #6. God sets appointed times and places by His authority. These are for you to meet with him and remember what He has done for you.

- ➢ Do you think Rehoboam had the authority to change these appointed times and places? Is there an appointed place to worship today? Do you or I have the authority to change the appointed times today? Why or why not?

- ➢ What days do you know of that are celebrated in different churches? If you find these days to not be in the Bible (Scripture), after you have learned about the authority of Scripture, then what should people do in this case? Do you think it is easy to change?

- ❖ **Statute Defined** (Choq or Chuqqah in Hebrew)- ordinance, appointed, fixed order; very similar in meaning to moedim. The word picture is of a wall representing a separation and a picture of the sun at the horizon which means to come together. [21] A Godly statute or ordinance brings a separated people together. God has set appointed statutes for us to follow. If we would obey His appointed statutes instead of making up our own, our church would represent the separated coming together. Gen. 1:14-15, Leviticus 23:31, Jeremiah 31:35-36

8. To recap what is happening, you have the 2 tribes under Jeroboam in the South (House of Judah), _____and _____. 12:21.

Then you have the other 10 tribes from the North (House of Israel) under Rehoboam. For some historical perspective up to this point and through the kings and prophets, check this out- *http://www.padfield.com/acrobat/harbison/kings-and-prophets-rh.pdf.*

- • From now on, the kingdom is divided into these 2 houses and this takes place about **931 BC,** which means that if you look at the approximately 6000 years of history we have that takes us back to Genesis, this is about 3000 years from creation.

- • Over the remainder of 1 and 2 Kings, you will see a few good kings and many evil ones.

- ➢ **Time to write in your Bible**. You have been through enough lessons now and are growing in your study skills. Take a blue pen and mark King #1, 2, 3 and so on beside each king for the Kingdom of Judah (southern). Take a red pen and mark King #1, 2, and so on for each king for the Kingdom of Israel (northern) as you come to them in the text. (Yes, you may "Google" kings of Israel and Judah to get some help as you are reading). I am telling you this because this is your history, your salvation, and the more you begin to interact with the Living Word of God, the more real and alive it will become to you. My Bible is all marked up, not to think I am better than someone else, but because I want to know and remember all I can about God so that it will change my life.

9. _____ the prophet arrives to give a Word from God to King Ahab. 17:1.

- • What kind of king was Ahab and who was his wife? 16:30-33

10. You need to read chapter 18 now. The reason that I continue to ask you to read certain chapters ahead of answering the questions is that it reads as a story or narrative. If you do not it is like trying to watch a movie for the first time and only watching scenes 1, 5, 7, and 12 instead of watching all 12 at once.

- A battle is about to take place between God and the false gods just like with Pharaoh and Egypt. In this case, Elijah the prophet of God asks Ahab to gather the 450 prophets of _____ and the 400 prophets of <u>Asherah</u> and meet him at Mt. Carmel.

- Elijah presents a truth challenge to see the condition of their _____ and he asks, "how long will you go limping between two _____ opinions.

- Will God share you, his child, with another God? Exo. 20:3-4, 34:14. This is not a petty jealousy like you may have over your boyfriend/girlfriend, but a zealous righteous love for you, his child!

- Elijah mocks the god Baal while waiting for him to respond. He says, Cry aloud for he is a god. Maybe he is thinking (musing), or going to the bathroom, or is on a _____, or he is _____.

  > **Nature of God**: This brings up a great theological (study of God) question. Does the God of the universe have to think (muse) about what to do, go to the bathroom, or only be in one place at a time? Is God limited or confined like a human by his own creation? Read Psalm 147:5, Rom. 11:33, John 4:24, Psalm 139:8-10.

- What did Elijah build to the LORD and how many times did they soak it with water and then what happens next?

- How did God respond compared to how Baal responded? What happened to all the false prophets?

- Elijah thought he was the only one that had not forsaken the _____ of God. 19:9-10. How many had not worshipped the Ba'al gods?

> ➤ **Extreme Thought**: What lesson can you learn when you think that you are the only one who is walking according to God, you are the only one making tough decisions that make you stand out, and the only one obeying your parents? Are you ready to stand for the minority position of truth in the culture? Can you think of any cultural issues right now?

11. Since this is discipleship curriculum, then it would be good to talk a little about a great example from 1 Kings 19:19, Elijah will begin to disciple Elisha so he can become the next prophet to speak for the LORD.

- Who did Elisha leave in order to learn the ways of being a prophet of the LORD? 19:20. The Messiah Jesus, God's only Son, teaches about this in Luke 14:26-27.

- When you read the verse from Luke, you may ask, "Why would Jesus ask me to hate my own family." This word does not mean hate as if they are worthless and evil, but compared to the love that you are to have for Jesus, your love for your family will seem like hate. To use correct biblical understanding of these terms, this means God is loyal to one and disloyal to the other. Why would God be loyal to one who rejects Him and His ways? Why would God drag someone into His kingdom that wants nothing to do with Him or His commands? And for us, we must forgive the individual, but we never forget iniquity and the danger that it holds for each of us. If we have to separate ourselves from that person, we must do it. Our love must seem like hate towards them compared to our love for God. This is not contradictory or opposite, but you are following the ways of God and the salvation in you. See Lesson 16 #11 and remember the context and that your love for God always comes first. I know this can be hard to grasp, but keep thinking about it and what He did for you at the cross. Philippians 2:8.

12. In 22:1-3, it says that Syria and Israel continued without _____. You have not heard the last of wicked King Ahab so let us see what happens next. King Ahab and King Jehoshaphat of Judah, meet together to go fight <u>Syria</u> for the land of Ramoth-Gilead.

- Jehoshaphat tells Ahab, the King Israel that it would be wise to inquire first for the

    _____ of the LORD. Ahab then gathers all 400 _____ together to see if

    they should go to war. They said go and take it and the LORD will be with you, but

    Jehoshaphat asks if there is another prophet and Ahab says yes there is Micaiah but I

    _____ him for he never prophesies _____ concerning me, but only _____ .

- Do you think Micaiah had heard about the evil of Ahab?

- Micaiah is told as he is being led to the king that the other 400 prophets are in _____ . There is so much pressure to tell the truth and now he gets this news.

- When he is first asked by Ahab to go to war or not, what does Micaiah tell him? 22:14-16

- Ahab knew he was lying, so use your imagination and just think of how Micaiah must have said it that it was so obvious he was lying. Was there some sarcasm in his voice, did his body language give him away? (I will continue to ask you questions like this even though you cannot know for sure. It is okay to put yourself into their lives). Please remember that these are real people who have emotions like joy, laughter, anger and who struggle with an evil inclination (sin) just like we all do.

  ➢ Take a moment and think about what it would be like to stand up against your whole school, (maybe your class has 400), and you are the only one that tells the truth. What names will they call you? Remember you serve the only true God, the creator of the universe- Isaiah 44:1-8.

  ➢ **Extreme Thought:** So many young people talk a big talk about being rebellious and all tough, but then they follow the crowd or keep to themselves because they don't need anybody (as if this is really true). This does not make you a rebel. This makes you a loner or a follower, letting others lead and you are just along for the ride. Let Jesus Christ lead you into all truth and follow this even if you are the only one! This way you are never alone and later others will follow Him through you. Are there any rappers out there? See what you can do with this and let me hear it sometime, all right? Don't forget me when you become famous.
- You are at the end of 1 Kings and there have been 4 kings for Judah in the south and 8 kings for Israel in the North. See the pattern for good and evil in 1 Kings 22:43, 52.

13. Elisha refuses to leave his master, his discipler. In this culture, to use the term "master" it meant mentor or teacher and later the Jewish term would be master or rabbi. To sit under a master did not mean you were a slave or that you were not worthy of anything. He stayed with him and had one last request, "Please let there be a _____portion of your spirit on me." 2 Kings 2:6-9.

- This is true discipleship, because there was nothing more important than receiving the blessing of the double portion. Elisha desired to be a prophet and walk in righteousness more than anything. May God raise up more men and women from each generation that will walk with this same desire to love the LORD by walking in His ways.
- Elijah never died, but left by a _____into heaven. 2:10-14.

14. In chapters 2-13, you can read that Elisha did twice as many miracles as did Elijah. Could that have been part of that double portion? Elisha dies and what happened when the grave robbers touched his bones? 13:20-21. Yes, grave robbers are actually in the Bible.

➤ Hollywood could make great movies like this without all the evil speech, nudity, etc. But they choose to walk in unrighteousness. What movies do you watch and how do you decide what you should watch? Is the Bible your guide?

15. At this time in our history, two prophets, **Amos and Hosea** are given a word from the LORD and they come to Israel and ask the people to repent. Amos and Hosea are books in your bible in the "prophet section." Read these two books or at least read the first 2 chapters of each to get some context.

- In Hosea 1:1, what king of Israel did Hosea prophesy to?

- In Hosea 4:1-6, list at least 3 reasons why they are prophesying against the people of Israel.

- In Amos 1:1, what king is Amos talking to? 2 Kings 14:23.

- In Amos 3:10, you can see why God sent Amos with His words.

A. Memory Verse: I Kings 11:6 (Write it out here).

B. Okay it is your turn to come up with good questions, using the format I have given you. You can do it. No worries!

1.

2.

3.

4.

5.

6.

C. Application How does this biblical truth affect how I live my life each day? Does this explain what you see in the news each day or what you see in your family and friends?

D. Journal and prayer time. Is there a sin you need to confess? Ask God to help you live according to what you have just studied. Praise Him today.

Lesson 17: A House Divided Against Itself Cannot Stand   (2 Kings and the Prophets)

You just finished lesson 16, which was over 300 years of historical truth. The last lesson and the next two will be a little longer. I know you are still missing a lot of details, but you are getting a good foundation of the Bible and then you can build upon it next year. Remember the goal is not to say, "I finished and learned some cool facts" but to say, "God is awesome and I want to serve Him because He has given me true hope for each day and all of eternity." The reason I chose the title for this lesson is because the LORD called his people to walk in righteousness, yet almost all of their kings did what was evil before Him. God allowed them to live this way for a little while, which displays His amazing grace, but He is also a just God. Therefore, their sin could not continually go unpunished. I pray that you are excited to get to the next lesson and that you are reading ahead in the Bible. I want you to realize that the Bible applies to your life in so many ways. Do not read it as if it is just irrelevant ancient history, but that it is about your history because you have been grafted into the nation of Israel. I will teach you more about this later. Okay, no more delays. It is time to see what happens while the prophets *Hosea, Amos, Isaiah and Micah* are bringing their messages from God primarily to the *Northern tribes (Israel)* and *Zephaniah, Jeremiah, Ezekiel and Habakkuk* prophesy what is to come for the *Southern tribes (Judah).*

1. Why did the northern kingdom of Israel fall? 2 Kings 17:3-12. See verse 12 for the main reason, but there were many reasons.

- Who was the last king of Israel (over the 10 tribes)? 15:27-30

- Hosea and Amos warned some of the kings and the people, but they did not listen. See Hosea 5:13, 8:9, 11:5, Amos 5:24-26.

- What happened to the people of Israel? 17:6

- _____takes over _____, the capitol of Israel. This is about 722 BC. 2 Kings 17:24

2. An interesting event happens next that I will not explain in great detail, but it is worth mentioning. _____, the king of _____, takes the Israelites out of their land and inhabits the land with people from other nations. The LORD sends lions in to kill the people because they do not belong to that piece of _____.   2 Kings 18:13, 17:24-26.

- The king sends in an Israelite priest to teach them the _____of the God of the land. 17:26-28. Go back to Genesis 15:18-21, 26:3, 50:24, Exodus 6:8, 32:13, Numbers 11:12, Deuteronomy 1:8, Joshua 1:6. There is something sacred about that piece of land then and it is still sacred today. God began everything in this place and when the Messiah, Jesus returns a second time, it will be to rule and reign from that piece of land. I am talking about Jerusalem in Israel. Do not think for one moment that what is happening in the Middle East is about politics. It is about religion, it is about "my God against your god." Some things will never change until Y'shua (Jesus) returns. Revelation 21:1-8.

- In 2 Kings 17:29-33, the people listened to the priest. T or F

- Is it okay to serve the LORD and other gods? Exodus 20, Deuteronomy 5.

3. The king of Assyria prepares to attack Judah, the last two tribes that remained. King Hezekiah did what was _____in the eyes of the LORD. 18:1-3.

- What nation had Judah put their trust in? 18:20-21

- What is the attitude of King Sennacherib of Assyria? 18:18-33

- The king of Assyria came to _____ the true living God. 19:4

- The king of Judah, _____ seeks the counsel of the prophet
  _____. 19:3

- The prophet responds by saying that the King of Assyria will retreat and _____. 19:7

- Hezekiah (13th king of Judah) knows that he must _____and seek God's favor. 19:14-16

  ➢ So even though Hezekiah heard the good news from the prophet Isaiah, he still prays to the LORD to guide him. What does that tell you about our call to pray when in need?

- What 2 major events happened in 19:35-37?

- Hezekiah is sick and he prays and the LORD answers by giving him _____more years of life. 20:1-6.

- Isaiah told Hezekiah the future (he prophesied) and that the nation of Judah will be carried off by the nation of _____ 20:13-19

4. _____, the 16th king of Judah did what was right in the eyes of the LORD. 22:2

- The new king makes plans to restore the _____ 22:3-4. Do you remember why that is so important? (Hint: Who dwells there?

- What treasure does Hilkiah the priest find in the temple? 22:8-9

- After it is read to King Josiah, he immediately _____ his clothes and commands the _____ to inquire of the LORD. 22:10-13

- Josiah knows that the _____ of the LORD is against them because of the disobedience of their _____. 22:13

  ➤ **Extreme Thought!** Did you notice that Josiah, after 600 years without the Word of God does not check with the current leaders or cultural trends (what is popular or politically correct in society or among the religious leaders), but says, "we need to obey all of God's commands"? How can you apply this to your life today?

- Hilkiah the priest and other leaders went to seek after Huldah the _____. Yes ladies can serve God in this way too.

- What main two things does Huldah prophesy about concerning the nation of Judah and about Josiah? 22:17-20

- Josiah reads all the words of the _____ of the _____ that was found, to the people and then he enters back into the _____ with God. 23:1-4

- Did God ever break the covenant?

- What important "appointed time" does Josiah restore that had not been obeyed in over 600 years? 23:21-23, Exodus 12, Leviticus 23.

- Do you see some patterns of disobedience? Go back to Deuteronomy 8:18-20

5. God had spared the nation of Judah (gracious God) and despite prophetic statements and warnings from the following prophets, they still did not repent as a nation. Zephaniah 1:1-5, Jeremiah 1:1-5, 18, Habakkuk 1:5-6, 12.

- In Habakkuk chapter 1, you see that the LORD is a just God and He is using an evil nation, the _____, to bring judgment upon His people so that they will _____(turn back to what is righteous).

- How does Habakkuk respond in 3:17-19 despite his struggles with what will happen for many of the people?

  - ➢ **Needs vs. Wants**: God is a covenant God that will always provide the needs of His people. He does not say he will always provide our wants. Take a moment and write down your basic needs in life. Also ask yourself, "Will I rejoice when the world looks dark and hopeless, when my life's situations seem to be getting the best of me?"

- In 24:1-4, you see that the LORD would tolerate no more and allows Judah to be completely taken over in 586 BC by _____under King Nebuchadnezzar.

- In 2 Kings chapters 24 and 25, you see the last 3 kings over Judah and they were Jehoiakim, Jehoiachin (also knows as Jeconiah or Coniah) and _____.

- What happens to Jehoiachin in 25:27?

- Why is this so important? Matthew 1:11, 16

6. Read the book of Daniel now if you can. It is a great book with many powerful stories to teach us about the LORD. The people of Judah are carried off into captivity under King Nebuchadnezzar. He is taking all the young men and training them. Daniel 1:1-6.

➢ Why do you think that the King of Babylon would be taking the people out of their land, teaching them his ways, and changing their names?

• God sends the prophets Daniel and Ezekiel during this time to give the people some encouragement to know that things would get better.

• Daniel fears the LORD and he trust His God, so he tells the chief of the eunuchs that he

will not defile himself with the king's food and will only eat _____ and

drink _____for 10 days and see what will happen to our appearance compared to

the others.

➢ **Extreme Thought: Trusting God In All Things**: The primary issue here is a spiritual issue, but there is a physical one as well. All spiritual things in your life take place in a physical body, so the two cannot be separated as if one has no importance. And you are thinking that when your parents say "vegetables will make you healthy and strong" they are just making it up. Are you taking good care of your temple in our day of fast food, processed food, GMO, GE and preservatives? What choices are you making and does God care about this part of your life as well?

• Why did Daniel say this? Acts 21:25, Exo. 24:15, Daniel 1:8.

7. King Nebuchadnezzar has a dream and wants it interpreted, but there is one thing different than any other narrative about interpreting a dream. He wants someone to tell him his _____ and then _____ it. He is going to kill every wise man if they cannot do so.

• Just as God raises up Joseph, he raises up Daniel, <u>Hananiah</u>, <u>Mishael</u>, and <u>Azariah</u>. The last 3 are more commonly known by their Babylonian names as Shadrach, Meshach, and Abednego. God gives Daniel the gift of understanding dreams and visions.

• In Chapter 2, Daniel tells the king his dream and the interpretation. After this, the king

says, "Truly your God is _____of gods and Lord of _____. 2:47.

• In chapter 3, the king declares that anyone who does not bow down and

_____the gold statue of the king will be burned in the furnace. Of course,

Daniel and his 3 friends will not bow and thus Daniel's 3 friends are thrown into the fire.

- Daniel and his 3 companions tell the king, "And our God will deliver us out of your hand, but if not, let it be known that we will _____ serve your gods or _____ the golden image you have set up." Exodus 20:3-4, Daniel 3:18-19.

  ➢ As you understand your faith more by studying more and being taught by men and women that love the LORD, you will find yourself asking questions like, "Would I stand up like this with such bold faith?"

- Even after seeing these great miracles, the king would fall because he was _____. _____ is the root of all sins because you must be humble to approach God. You can never think that you are above God. 1 Peter 5:5.

  ➢ **Pride:** I want you to think very carefully about your life. Where are your prideful areas? Take a serious look, repent and ask others to keep you accountable in these areas so you will change. It is better to change now than to wait for 10-20 years. The longer you do it, the tougher it is to change. Just ask your parents or your pastor if this is true.

8. Another king comes to power. What was his name and what brought him to ruin? Daniel 5:1-5, 22-24.

- What message does he receive from God in 5:24-30?

A. Memory Verse: Proverbs 21:1-2 (Write it out here).

B. Six questions to ask while thinking back through the text.

1. Who found the Book of the Law?

2. What did Josiah do when he found out?

3. When did he repent?

4. Where was the Book of the Law found?

5. Why did he repent?

6. How did he decide if he should obey?

C. Application How does this biblical truth affect how I live my life each day? Does this explain what you see in the news each day or what you see in your family and friends? Praise God for helping you to see His ways over your own ways and thoughts.

D. Journal and prayer time. Is there a sin you need to confess? As you do this, ask God to help you live according to what you have studied. Praise Him today.

Lesson 18: Will Any of God's People Return? (Ezra, Nehemiah and Esther)

Have you continued the habit of highlighting, underlining, etc. in your Bible? I pray so because this shows that you are becoming a student of the Word. Wherever you are on this, be encouraged that God wants to meet with you in all your efforts to grow closer to Him. I know you have noticed that I continually skip some books of the Bible (God's Word), but if I did not skip some books, this would be 52 lessons instead of 26. Trust me; the more you grow in this journey of salvation, the more you will realize the depths of the Word which is the depths of God. There is no separation between the Word of God and God. The Word of God (the Bible, the scriptures) emanates (to come or send forth, as from a source) from God's very character and nature. If you say you do not want to study God's Word then you do not want to be with God. You cannot say I love God but do not want to be in His Word. That is a contradiction in God's eyes.

I know you may not understand this totally, but just keep studying the Word and let God transform you and give you a desire to love Him more. Psalm 19:10. Last, if you will make it a priority, you could read the other books while you are going through this so you don't have to miss anything. However, if you are not able to do so, I pray that at some point you will take the time to finish reading God's beautiful words of life.

I have chosen this title for this section of study because it is the end of the reign of the Babylonians that was prophesied by the prophet Jeremiah (Jeremiah 25:12-15) and now a remnant (minority of people) will come back and serve the LORD again (Ezra 9:8). With this return comes two difficult tasks—rebuilding the temple and rebuilding the walls of the city of Zion or Jerusalem. As you do this lesson, you will realize just how hard this was.

Before you get to the events of the return of the exile or remnant, there is one more event in Daniel's life that is worth mentioning and it transitions us from the Babylonians to the next great empire. King Darius is the first king of the Medo-Persian kingdom (Medes and Persians) and thus he begins to appoint rulers under him. Of course Daniel becomes second in power in this empire. Does this sound like Joseph's story? God takes care of his people. Now the story shows us there are some plotters or whiners (as I like to call them). There are always people in this world that will complain about anything or anybody. They plot to trap Daniel. Read Daniel 6:1-9.

- Once Daniel heard about this decree from the king, he immediately stopped worshipping the LORD. T or F   Daniel 6:10-13

- What happens next to Daniel? 6:14-17

- What decree did the king make after this great event? 6:18-28

1. In Ezra 1:1-5, what is happening?

- What tribes return to participate in this event? What is significant about two of the three tribes?

- Is Cyrus, the King of Persia, an Israelite or a believer in the LORD? What does Proverbs 21:1-2 and Psalm 95:3 tell you that helps explain what is happening? This was your last memory verse, so you got this.

- King Cyrus even gives God's people the stolen items of king Nebuchadnezzar, (2 Chronicles 36:7) to put back in the _____ once it is built. Also read Isaiah 44:24-45:7.

2. In chapter 3, when all the people had come back, did they return to doing things their way or God's way? Name a few from verses 4-5?

- In 3:6-8, _____ is the one who supervises the building of the temple?

- Why was it a big deal that the temple was in ruins? Do you remember what the temple represented?

- Why do you think some of the old men wept when they saw the new temple foundation? 3:12

- In Ezra 4:1 you read, "Now the _____ of Judah and Benjamin heard that the returned exiles (remnant) were building a temple to the LORD God and wanted to _____. They were told that they could not help. Ever since Adam and Eve sinned, there will always be good and evil.

- What do these troublemakers do because they are not allowed to help? 4:4-8, 13-15

- The new king is king Artexerxes and he makes the decree.

- What came of the building of the temple after this? 4:24

3. It is prophet time! They are almost like superheroes but without capes. Actually, they were in the desert and needed protection from the sun, so they might have had "capes." The prophets _____ and _____ give them a message. What is it?

4. In 6:1-5, what does King Darius find and how are things now changed?

- How serious is King Darius about making this right? 6:11

- ➤ **Understanding Context and Ancient Culture**: You may be reading this and think that is a cool story, but this is even more amazing that you realize. For a king of a conquering nation to allow a nation to rebuild its temple and pay for it, was something that just did not happen. God is in control and on top of all of this, he does this under a nation that makes decrees that cannot be broken even by another king. So the decree of Cyrus overrides the decree of Artexerxes. All of these details are amazing. We serve a great God. Ezra 7:27-28

5. What takes place in Ezra 6:14-15?

- What was now restored in 6:18? Numbers 3:6-8

- What is happening again and who led them in this? 7:10

- In 7:6, it talks about _____ "He was a scribe, skilled in the Law of Moses that the LORD, the God of Israel had given.

- Also in Luke 21:37, you will see that Jesus did the same thing. God will always use people to lead in this way.

  - ➤ **Critical Thought: Studying the Word-** Look at 7:6-10 and find three words that are necessary for you to become a student of the Word (skilled, study, and do). Do you think God will use you to teach and lead if you do not desire in your heart, his laws (teachings), his ways? Remember that you cannot separate your love for God from your love for His Word. As you look at the Bible, you will find that God does not ask you to read it, but to **study**, to meditate or think on it and to **do** (obey) it. It is not about reading the Bible that will grow you, although this is the beginning. To be **skilled** at anything takes time, so be patient and continue learning. The real reason you are doing this curriculum is to allow the Word of God to forever change your thoughts, actions, your whole life (Lesson 15 #17). Have you been studying the Word of God with this correct understanding? If not, begin today.

6. Ezra is a priest and the priests had many jobs, but they would all fall under these three principal duties before God: (See Lessons of Exodus and Leviticus).
- ✓ They were to guard and take care of the temple.
- ✓ They were to guard and take care of the people.
- ✓ They were to guard and take care of the Torah (teachings of God; His Word).

- In chapter 9, he had the duty of guarding the people and guarding the Torah, so he realizes that the people (God's chosen people) have "_____ themselves with the peoples of the land." 9:2. Do you remember the problem with mixing that goes all the way back to Garden of Eden in lesson 2 #4?

- Was the problem with intermarriage that God is a racist and only likes a certain race? Read Romans 9:4-5 and see the responsibility they had? Ezra 9:14.

- The people respond by doing two things. They recognize God's _____ and they come before God in their _____ (repent). 9:14-15 and 10:1.

- Next they say, "Let us make a _____ with our God to put away all these wives and their children, according to the counsel of my lord. 10:3

  - ➢ **Cultural Influence**: Do you think it was easy to be obedient at this point? You will find that as you learn more of God, then you are accountable to more before God. Think back when I asked you in Lesson 16 #7 if it would be easy to break away from church traditions that may not be obedient to God. Some church traditions are totally okay, even though the exact commandment is not found in the Scriptures. For example, if your church plays 4 songs and has two prayers every Sunday. This is not necessarily wrong, so this tradition may be okay as long as the heart of the leaders is right. Test all things against the heart of God (His Word).

7. The temple is built in 515 BC, but the city _____ lie in ruin, so God brings up _____, a man that loves Him to do this great task of protecting the temple and the people. Nehemiah 1:1-5

- God says if the people obey, He will bring back more of the exiles to dwell in His city. 1:8-9.
- Nehemiah seeks the favor of King Artexerxes and as God was with Ezra, He gives favor to Nehemiah. (it is ultimately God who gives favor). Exodus 33:13-17, Proverbs 21:1-2.

8. Here come the adversaries just like with Ezra and their names are _____ and _____. Nehemiah 2:9-10, 4:1-3, 6:1

- When things get tough, you better unite and trust in the LORD. This is what you see in 4:10-14. Nehemiah says, "Do not be afraid of them, Remember the LORD , who is great and awesome and fight for your _____, your _____, your _____, your _____and your _____."

- On top of these words, he also told them to build the wall with one hand and have your weapon in the other. Can you say prepared?

  ➤ This is a great picture of spiritual warfare. Know that when you become a disciple of Jesus Christ, some things are tougher and not easier. When you "rebel" against the popular culture (as I talked about earlier) it will be tough. You may be the only one fighting at certain times or certain places. Don't ever give up. <u>Read to see what Jesus says. John 10:28-29, 15:18-19, 16:33.</u>

9. In Nehemiah 6, the wall is finished in _____ days (445 BC). This may not sound like such a big deal, but when you consider that the historian Josephus tells us that inside the walls were 960 acres or close to 1.5 square miles, this was awesome. Not to mention, they had enemies plotting against them.

10. Do you realize that Nehemiah is an amazing leader and a great man of God? If you have not discovered this, please continue reading. **What makes a good leader?** <u>Read chapters 8-9.</u>

  ➤ He calls the people to observe all of God's _____. He does not just teach what is easy.

  ➤ He calls them to repentance and to _____(separation).

  ➤ He walks in _____ before them (sets the example).

11. _____is the first recorded preacher in the scriptures. He not only reads the Word to them, but with the help of others, _____ it to them. <u>Every good preacher will teach and preach..</u> 8:1-8

12. Read chapter 13 now. Nehemiah works to establish the priesthood, clean out those that have defiled the temple and call the people back to total repentance before God.

BOOK OF ESTHER

13. I am going to do a very quick summary of the book of Esther. I am only bringing in a couple of teaching moments, so if you want to follow you will need to read it. It is a great book and there was even a pretty good movie that came out about 7 years ago called One Night With the King.

- King Ahasuerus (Xerxes) is king over the Medo-Persian Empire.
- Queen Vashti refuses to come to the king when summoned so another _____ is sought from the lands.

- _____ (Hadassah is her Jewish name), the cousin of Mordecai ends up being chosen to be the queen of the land.
- _____ saved the king by stopping a plot that was against him. 2:22

- Haman, the Agagite is promoted by the king and he wants the king to decree to destroy all the Jews. Can you figure out from 1 Samuel 15:3-9 why he wants to do this and should this story even be here? Why do Agagites still exist?

- What have you learned about a decree in the Medo-Persian Empire from the book of Daniel?

- Esther asks that all Jews _____ and pray and she will approach the king without being summoned in order to reveal Haman. 4:15-17.

- **You get the privilege of finishing the narrative of Esther. Write out some thoughts even though I am not asking specific questions? You can do it.**

14. I am skipping the poetic books, which include Job (oldest book of the Bible), Psalms, Proverbs, Ecclesiastes, Song of Songs (Solomon) and Lamentations. I will continue to send you there to read certain verses, to get answers, etc., but that is it for this year. I will tell you that the Psalms teach much about prayer and about God's character. The Proverbs speak in very practical terms about what a man looks like when he walks in righteousness and what he looks like when he walks in wickedness.

A. Memory Verse: Ezra 7:27 (Write it out here).

B. Six questions to ask while thinking back through the text.

1. Who were the main characters in these three books?

2. What did Nehemiah do when he heard about Jerusalem?

3. When did he know it was time to go rebuild?

4. Where was Hadassah from?

5. Why did Nehemiah need to rebuild the walls?

6. How was this accomplished?

C. Application How does this biblical truth affect my life?

D. Journal and prayer time. Is there a sin you need to confess? As you do this, ask God to help you live according to what you have just studied. Praise Him for His many blessings.

Lesson 19: Will God Speak Again? (Intertestamental Period and the Gospels)

You are about to end what is called the Old Testament (OT) and enter into what is referred to as the New Testament (NT). Make sure you understand that just because the translators of the Bible decided to divide it into books and sections, the Bible is just one book with one central message: God is holy and sovereign and gives an opportunity for continual redemption (through Yeshua) from sin to those that truly repent. (also see Lesson 1 #1). He reveals Himself in many ways, including more revelation of grace and redemption for sinful man through the Messiah, Jesus Christ.

The beginning is the foundation for everything you will now see from Matthew to Revelation, which is why you are studying in chronological order. Remember Isaiah 46:10. The more you understand your history, the very beginning of God's redemptive story, the more you can build upon it. This will keep you true to the Word of God. God will now send His only Son to walk the Earth. I will refer back quite often during these next 8 lessons so that you can see the consistency, unity and grace of our God. He is the same from the beginning until the end. *Also, remember as you do these last few lessons, that all of these letters and books were written by Jewish authors that did not have a NT to look at or teach from. Salvation, repentance, worship, etc. was all taught from the truth of the Tanakh (OT), just as you have been taught these Godly principles in their original context.* These authors are not contradicting anything about God, His ways, or His salvation, but are building upon and teaching from these very same truths. These same authors also reference and quote from the OT numerous times in the NT.

The Tanakh (OT) ends in the book of Malachi with these words, "But for you who fear my name, the sun of righteousness shall rise with healing in its wings….. Remember the law of my servant Moses, the statutes and rules that I commanded him at Mt. Horeb for all Israel. Behold I will send you Elijah the prophet before the great and awesome Day of the LORD comes." The message from God is consistent. Here, he prophesies through Malachi that the Messiah will come, Elijah the prophet will come and that my people need to obey my laws in order to restore each family, and together restore the family of God. Are you seeing how consistent the Bible is at this point? You serve a God that will not change His character and cannot do so, thus be encouraged each day, as you can confidently trust Him.

The next 400 years was a period of time in which there was no revelation from God coming down through prophets. God's people had not listened when He spoke through the prophets and this was a time where the people had continual unrest concerning their identity, land, morality, and the priesthood. Within this culture, they had rejected their king (God) in many ways. The priesthood had become extremely corrupt and usually went to the highest bidder. There was however always a remnant of people that wanted to remain true to God and His commandments. This is the setting when John the Baptist (type of Elijah) and Yeshua are introduced in history. If you would like to read some great history during the next 400 years before the time of the NT takes place, then read the Apocrypha. This book is great for learning history during this time period, but there are some things in there that are not consistent with what is in God's Holy Word and thus were left out of the Bible. There are also some great men and women of God to read about during this time period from about 400 BC to when Yeshua (Jesus) comes to what is now referred to as A.D. During these 400 years, the Medo-Persian Empire fell and Alexander the Great led the Greek army to become the next great empire in 332BC. They eventually fell and were proceeded by the Roman Empire, which is the controlling nation during the time when the Messiah walks the earth. As always, I will encourage you to read as much as you can.

The next two lessons will cover the gospels (Matthew, Mark, Luke and John). These are four accounts of the life of Yeshua. I will refer often to Jesus as Yeshua, Y'hoshua or Y'shua. These are different spellings of Jesus' name in Aramaic or Hebrew and it was common for people to be referred to with two names. Y'hoshua is where we get Joshua and Yeshua or Y'shua is where we get Jesus through transliteration. A modern example of more than one name would be someone named Robert, but some people call him Bob. Since these Hebrew names mean to rescue, salvation or God is salvation, I prefer to use them. Jesus is an English transliteration from Hebrew or Aramaic, Greek, Latin and then English. Jesus does not mean salvation within the word Jesus itself, which is why I will usually use His Hebrew name, Yehoshua or shortened to Yeshua. Jesus is what you are used to seeing and if you still like to use Jesus, there is no problem with that. The last thing I will mention before beginning this section is the fact that the gospels are not completely chronological, but as with all Hebrew writings, the themes are more important than the chronology. Thus, I will not focus upon the chronological order as much as I have done up to this point. I will do this in more detail when I teach the gospels online at my website- only1way.net

1. Read Matthew 1:1-17 (also see Luke 3:23-38). Notice as you go through this genealogy, that it is not a list of people that never did anything wrong, but they are people just like you and me. They have sinned and God has forgiven them through His grace. This is the genealogy that shows you the coming Messiah, Yeshua (Jesus).

Every generation for about _____ _____ has been waiting for this day. **Do you understand how huge this is?**

2. Zechariah, the _____ from the division of Abijah is married to Elizabeth and she is

_____. Luke 1:5-7.

- What happens while Zechariah is serving in the temple? Luke 1:8-21

- Who does Zechariah sound like in Luke 1:18? Genesis 17:17 and Luke 1:37.

- An awesome thing happens in Luke 1:16, "he will be filled with the Holy Spirit, even from his mother's womb."

  ❖ **Holy Spirit defined**- (Ruach HaKodesh in Hebrew) God is spirit and not flesh like man. He reveals Himself in many ways including dwelling inside of man in order to accomplish His purposes. In the OT, the Holy Spirit was active in creation (Genesis 1:2), in building the temple (Exodus 31), in guiding some judges and kings (Judges 3:10 and 2 Samuel 23) and giving words through the prophets (Isaiah 61:1). The Holy Spirit is one and in perfect unity with God. The Holy Spirit or Spirit of God cannot do anything against God because He is one with God and was sent from God to reveal God's activity in the lives of His created beings in order to accomplish all of His purposes for His own glory. The only difference between the Holy Spirit in the OT and in the NT, is that in the NT he comes to permanently dwell (Ephesians 1:13, 2 Timothy 1:14, Romans 5:5) in a disciple of Yeshua (one who has salvation from God through Yeshua). However, there are examples previously of men who have walked continuously in the Spirit. He is also a helper and a comforter. God is always with you and in you as His Spirit abides in you! If you feel distant from God, then examine your life to find the sin, repent and you will find that the Spirit of God never left you.

- After the angel appears to Zechariah, he also appears to Mary to tell her about her

  upcoming birth. He tells her in 1:32, "And the LORD God will give to him the throne of

  his father _____, and he will reign over the house of _____ forever, and of

  his kingdom there will be no end." God is keeping his _____according to

  Genesis 35:11 and 2 Samuel 7:16.

3. Is there something supernatural about Mary's pregnancy? See Matthew 1:18-25. See Isaiah 7:14 for the prophecy of this moment. ("but knew her not" means he had not had sexual relations with her yet).

- Mary and Joseph were betrothed, which basically means that they were married in the eyes of everyone, including God, but the official wedding ceremony had not taken place. You might call that the engagement period, except in our culture, you can still just break it off and no big deal. If you broke off the betrothal, it was equal to getting a divorce.

- Where was Yeshua (Jesus) born and who was king? Also see Micah 5:2

- You will begin to notice the fulfillment of prophecies increasing as the Messiah (Yeshua) comes to the earth (which is His creation).

4. _____ the Baptist is born and after he is born, Zechariah is now able to _____ Luke 1:20, 57-64.

5. Why would this news of a king being born trouble king Herod? 2:6

6. What two things do the wise men do when they find the long-awaited Messiah? 2:11

7. How is the LORD protecting the Messiah in 2:12-22?

8. John the Baptist comes with a gospel message, which includes telling the people to

_____, for the kingdom of _____ is near, and they should

bear_____ (Ephesians 2:8-10, Genesis 1:28, Proverbs 11:30). Those fail to do so, will

be burned with unquenchable _____. Matthew 3:1-12.

- You will notice that the gospel message will be slightly different in certain passages in the Bible, but when put together you will realize it is a consistent message of truth. When studying the Bible, you will see in the future, the importance of knowing the context and the audience at the time of writing.

9. Yeshua has the Holy Spirit in him to guide him and he is led by the Spirit into the wilderness to be _____ by the devil. After fasting for 40 days, the devil (Satan) tempts him in three ways:

- ✓ "Command these stones to become loaves of bread" and Jesus replies by quoting Deuteronomy 8:3.
- ✓ "If you are the Son of God, throw yourself down and He will command his angels concerning you, and on their hands they will bear you up, lest you strike your foot against a stone." Jesus replies by quoting Deuteronomy 6:16
- ✓ "All these (kingdoms) I will give you, if you will fall down and worship me." Jesus answers by quoting Deut. 6:13.

- ➤ I want you to look up these verses from Deuteronomy and understand that no matter what you are going through, God's Word has an answer to protect you and guide you. Even God, revealed in His Son as a man (Jesus), knew that in his humanity, he needed to rely upon the truth of the Torah (God's instructions) for these temptations. <u>Does this help you understand why memorizing scripture is so important?</u>

10. There is only one place where you will see a chronological event of Yeshua growing up between his early years and the beginning of His ministry. In Luke 2:41-52, you see Yeshua at age 12 (age of Bar Mitzvah or age of accountability and responsibility as well as the beginning of manhood).

11. He is in Nazareth and he is preaching on the _____ (day 7 or Saturday) in the synagogue (building where they met to worship God through study, etc). In Luke 4:16-19, Jesus quotes from Isaiah 61:1-2 and it is being fulfilled through Him right then. Jesus begins his ministry and his gospel (good news) is the same as John the Baptist and all of the prophets. The message is to _____ Matthew 4:17.

12. Jesus calls the 12 apostles to follow him. He calls them at different times, but they are all listed here. Name the 12 found in Luke 6:12-16.

- In Matthew 4:19, he calls some of his first disciples (later will be called apostles). They are fishermen, but he wants them to be fishers of _____. Who are the men and women he is sending them to first? Jeremiah 16:14-16, Matthew 10:6, 15:24.

13. Yeshua (Jesus) is a Jewish (from the tribe of Judah) rabbi and you will see him teaching as rabbis did and still do. He _____ down and began to teach. He also taught from the Tanakh (Law, Prophets, and Writings or OT). There was no NT at this point. So when He taught about things like salvation, repentance, and prayer, He would have been teaching from the Tanakh (OT writings). Matthew 5:1, Luke 24:44.

- He begins to teach them what disciples will do and look like in 5:2-15. Disciples will be salt (make something taste better or be better) and light (a little light will overcome a lot of darkness).

  ➢ Are you living each day as salt and light? Are you being salt (making this world better) by living like Jesus and are you spreading light (righteousness) in a dark (unrighteous) world?

14. Read Matthew 5:17-19 now. Yeshua teaches some extremely important things here.

  ✓ Yeshua did not come to abolish the Law or Prophets, but to fulfill (In Greek, it is to fill up or make whole as if something was missing) The heart of God was in the law, but a small group of powerful Pharisee and Sadducee leaders had turned the Law into simply a bunch of rules and regulations. The heart of the law was now missing. You are also seeing a Hebrew idiom in which "to abolish or destroy" was to misinterpret and "to fulfill" meant to correctly interpret. Always remember that translating from one language to another involves not only the difficulty of finding the right word or phrase, but also understanding the complete cultural view of the world, as well as the idioms that would have only made sense to that culture.
  ✓ Not one grammatical marking or one letter of the Law or the Prophets' writings shall pass away until heaven and earth pass away, which means never.
  ✓ Nothing will be abolished (turned away or destroyed) until all is accomplished.
  ✓ If you put aside a commandment and teach others to do the same, you will be least in the kingdom, but if you do the opposite you will be great in the kingdom.

- Yeshua is saying that it is very important that you pay attention to every word that is in the Law and the Prophets. (reference to the OT writings). Also, you need to obey them and teach others to obey them. He also says that there are still things to come that have not been accomplished. As you are reading this and Yeshua the Messiah has not come back a second time, then all is not accomplished.

15. Finish reading Matthew chapters 5-7 (Sermon on the Mount). Yeshua is teaching them the heart of the Law (instructions of God). You will notice this is always about what motivates you to do something (the condition of your heart). Read Matthew 6:9-15 and Luke 11:1-4. Notice that prayer is something that will continuously be _____. After all, these men had grown up praying.

> ➢ How is the condition of your heart as you wake up each morning, as you listen or do not listen to your parents, as you respect or do not respect your parents, as you go to school, as you go to work, as you are on the computer?

> ➢ Will you take the time to grow in your prayer life? Prayer is not about talking and giving God a bunch of "I want's" but it is about talking and listening. For some of you, this seems strange since God does not talk to you where you can hear Him. However, if you are a disciple of Jesus Christ, then you have the Holy Spirit dwelling in you, which will guide you to all truth and this guidance will always agree with the Bible. As you grow, you will begin to hear Him speak (not audibly).

> ❖ **Prayer defined**- *Palal* in Hebrew literally means "speak to authority" so you are speaking to God who is the authority of all things, including you. It also means to plead or intercede, make request, supplication (humility before God). [22] You must know that you are speaking to a Holy God as you have learned and you cannot just come with a bad attitude and a prideful heart. You must come before Him in humility, asking for forgiveness (repentance), so that He will answer your prayers and restore you to righteousness. <u>God will not answer the prayer of a prideful heart!</u>

16. In Matthew 6:25-34, Yeshua says, "do not be _____ about your life, what you will _____ or drink, not about your body, what you will put on. Is not life more than food, and the body more than _____? Instead of worrying, "seek first the kingdom of God and his righteousness, and all these things will be added to you." Learn this verse- Matthew 6:33.

> ➢ What are the 5 basic needs of life?

> ➢ How much time do you spend worrying about these things? Who are you trying to impress?

17. As you continue to read through the gospels, you will notice that Jesus does many miracles, including healing many people. Jesus lived a life where he travelled to different cities, he taught in the synagogues (place of worship), and he interacted with many people. As people heard about his miracles, he became very popular, so he had crowds of people following him. They either wanted to be healed, want to see miracles, and/or they thought he was the Messiah. I will list a few miracles below with certain thoughts that will help. Remember that Jesus did not do miracles for entertainment or just for the sake of doing so. There was always a <u>spiritual purpose</u> that went along with the <u>physical</u> event.

✓ The faith of the centurion is found in Matthew 8:5-13- this healing emphasizes that faith is about the one whom we put our faith in and it is about action. This man belonged to the Roman army and yet he understood _____.

✓ Yeshua heals a paralytic in Matthew 9:1-8. Notice that Yeshua does not say you are healed, but says your sins are _____. Does this mean that the man's sins caused him to be paralyzed? Not necessarily, but we all live in a sinful world until Yeshua returns, thus there will always be some connection between the physical and spiritual. God gave his Son the authority to forgive sins and the people were afraid.

✓ Yeshua feeds 5000 men plus women and children. He only had ____loaves and _____ fish. They end up with _____basketfuls after they eat. He is continually doing things that show His relationship to the Father. Just as the LORD brought manna and quail down from heaven, Yeshua thanks God and has enough to feed this large crowd. John 6:1-15, 49-51

✓ Yeshua walks on _____ in Matthew 14:22-33. He is in control of the laws of nature that He set in place at the time of Creation from Genesis 1. Remember there is no mother nature, but only Father God. (Interesting how tradition can trump over truth).

✓ Yeshua heals a man who was born blind in John chapter 9. He performed this miracle on the _____(9:14) and this always made the Pharisee and Sadducee leaders angry. Some of the Pharisaic leaders had forgotten what the Torah (laws or instructions of God) was all about. They had added a bunch of extra laws that were not from God so the Sabbath became a time where you could do almost nothing. Jesus taught that you were to obey the Sabbath (See Leviticus 23 for the 7 appointed times to be obeyed), but there were times when it would be necessary to do good deeds on the Sabbath and so he did things like heal a blind man. Luke 6:9, Matthew 12:8-21.

➢ Maybe you are saying to yourself, "we are to obey the Sabbath as part of the appointed times, but now there are exceptions, so I am confused." Yeshua was not saying that every Sabbath you are to go and help people, thus neglecting His perfect plan of physical and spiritual restoration. Sabbath means a time of renewal set aside by Gode each week. See, many people get very busy today and thus ignore rest. This is why many pastors and ministry leaders get burned out, quit or end up in the hospital at an early age. This is why heart attacks and heart disease are on the rise. You must take care of your relationship with God on His times before you can help others. The Sabbath is the perfect cure for stress. God has primarily designed the Sabbath for spiritual rest, a day appointed by God, for you to reconnect with Him and your family without the stresses of work. You are commanded to keep this day holy (set apart) and there are times when you will help others. Be obedient, take care of your self and family and then you will be prepared and prioritized to help others. This way you are obeying what God meant by the command. Our example is seen in the fact that Yeshua never disobeyed the heart of the Sabbath. Many people will point to Luke 13:10-18 to say he broke the Sabbath but they misunderstood this crucial point. Obeying Torah is about life, not death. Whenever a chance to heal comes in conflict with allowing death, healing of life is chosen. Thus Yeshua obeyed Sabbath as it was intended. Obedience to any of God's commands does not come without using wisdom. Yes, you obey, but look at God's heart in the matter. Matthew 12:8-12, Mark 2:27-28.

A. Memory Verse: John 3:16-18. I know that this is a longer memory verse, but take the time to learn it all. I know you can do it.

B. Six questions to ask while thinking back through the text.

1. Who came before to announce the Messiah?

2. What was his gospel message?

3. When did Satan come to tempt Jesus?

4. Where was he while being tempted?

5. Why did God send His son Yeshua to become a man? Luke 4:43, Matthew 10:6, 34, 15:24, Luke 1:16, 24:21, John 6:38, 18:37, Romans 1:16.

6. How did Jesus fight off Satan?

C. Application How does this biblical truth affect me each day?

D. Journal and prayer time. Is there a sin you need to confess? As you do this, ask God to help you live according to what you have just studied? Praise God for loving us so much that He sent His only Son to die for us.

Lesson 20: The Messiah Has Come (Gospel of John)

Read the gospel of John before beginning this lesson, or at least read the first 4 chapters and then read some more each day. If you just fill in some occasional blanks, you will miss some of the meaning. Can you believe after several thousand years, the Messiah, the Anointed One, Yeshua is finally here? He is walking the earth and proclaiming who He is and why He came. This lesson will primarily focus on the life of Yeshua (Jesus) from the perspective of his disciple named John. He wrote the gospel of John, 1, 2, 3 John and Revelation from the Bible. He was referred to as the beloved one and was part of the three closest disciples to Jesus—Peter, James and John. John writes his gospel to cover many things, but his biggest focus is to state that Yeshua is the Messiah and the Son (Messiah) was one with the Father. This word "one" is the Hebrew word *echad*, which you learned about when studying Deuteronomy 6:4-9. This passage in scripture is referred to as the Shema (to hear and obey). Faith is about hearing and obeying. Being a disciple is about hearing and obeying. I know that you have learned so much up to this point and I also know that there will be many things you will forget and many things that you will pick up later. Either way, it is okay. Just stick with it and pray each day that God will draw you closer as you do each lesson. You will learn more about who He is and what this means to your daily walk with Him.

1. John 1:1-2- "In the beginning was the Word and the Word was with God and the Word was God." Does this remind you of Genesis 1:1?

- This verse can seem a little confusing. It is hard for us sometimes because we are sinful, we are human and thus do not understand everything about God. God is the Word (Torah or His words), God is truth, God is light, God is love, God is just, and God is grace. He does not try to be any of these, but He is all of these all the time. So Jesus is the Son of God, sent from God, to do God's will. Jesus is one with God as the Son (the Vassal King sent under the authority of the King of the Universe), the Messiah who has been revealed by God. He is also the Word (from the beginning), the truth, the good seed, etc. All the characteristics that are in God are in the Son, as He is emanated (come forth or out of), the Father, but not lesser or separate from the Father. We do not serve multiple gods, but only the one true God, your Creator.

- As he was on the earth, he was the walking Word, the walking truth, the walking light, the walking love, justice and grace. Wow! He is not the Father, but is one (echad) in character and nature with the Father. He perfectly obeys the Father and is one with the Father. All the characteristics that are in God are in the Son, as the Son walked in the power of the Holy Spirit while on earth. Yeshua was in the beginning with the Father, participated in creation (Colossians 1:16-17), has always existed, gave up His own life on the cross, but there is still only one God (Isaiah 44:6-8). Does your head hurt? Welcome to the world of theology (study of God). As you study, you are gaining knowledge, but this is not about knowledge for the sake of having more knowledge, but for learning more about God so you love Him more and worship Him daily.

2. John the Baptist came, fulfilling the prophecy from Isaiah. 1:19-34

- John was a spiritual type of Elijah, but he was not physically Elijah, raised from the dead.

- John came for the purpose of _____ with water that Yeshua might be revealed to _____.

- John points out that Yeshua is the Lamb of God. Exodus 12:5, 2 Chronicles 35:1-12, Ezra 6:20.

3. Yeshua performs his first sign or miracle by turning water into _____. John 2:1-11.

4. Why was Yeshua so upset in John 3:13-22? (Hint: This is God's house). Jesus was the walking temple of God. Everything in Him could only obey the Father and the Law of his Father's house. What miracle does he prophesy about in 3:18-22?

5. In John 3:1-15, Yeshua meets with _____, a Pharisee leader, and explains to him that you must be born from above in order to enter the kingdom of heaven. Yeshua is letting him know that what you do here only matters if you are part of the _____ of God. He continues in verses 16-21 to teach what separates the righteous from the unrighteous (the difference between one who seeks the light and the one who seeks the darkness). Do these verses sound familiar? Yes this was your memory verse from last week.

6. Yeshua does something totally against the culture of the day in two different ways (John 4:1-31). He talks alone with a woman and on top of that, a _____ woman. Samaritans were half-breeds, meaning they were Israelites that had mixed with other nations in disobedience. How do his disciples react in 4:27?

7. Yeshua is consistent throughout his life as he says, "I can do nothing on my own. As I hear, I judge, and my judgment is just, because I seek not my own _____ but the will of him (Father) who sent me." The Son does the _____ will. John 5:30, 6:38, 7:18, 28, 8:28, 42.

8. In John 5:48, many will not believe that he is the Messiah, so he points them back to the Torah, or Pentateuch in Greek (first 5 books of Bible) that was written by Moses. You can also see the OT (Tanakh) which means the Law, the _____, and the Writings (Luke 24:44). Also see Acts 7:37, Deuteronomy 18:15, 18.

9. To continue on this idea that the Messiah was spoken of in the OT, Yeshua calls himself the Bread of _____. In John 6:32, 45-51, he compares himself to the manna from heaven that was given to the Israelites in the desert (Exodus 16).

- As I have pointed out from the first lessons, everyone was looking for the Messiah and the OT spoke of the Messiah in so many different ways. The manna was physical, but it points to a spiritual meaning. There are more to come.
- Yeshua was the Bread of Life that gives life eternal.

10. After Yeshua said some harsh words that many did not understand in John 6, many people quit following him. He then asks his 12 apostles, "Do you want to go away as well?" What did Peter say?

11. What "_____ _____" or feast are they celebrating in John 7? See Leviticus 23 for the answer. Will this appointed time be celebrated when Yeshua returns to reign on earth? Zechariah 14.

12. In John 7:25-27, they are asking if he is the _____ (anointed one, Messiah)? He is doing miracles, saying things that were prophesied about him, and so they think it might be him.

13. In John 7:35, they are confused by Yeshua's words and they ask if he will go teach those of the _____ (the 10 tribes of Israel—The northern kingdom). After the 70 years of captivity, these 10 tribes never came back, but mixed into the culture. They would have been mixed into the Greco- Roman culture, but there was still distinction enough to know they were around. Yeshua came first for the Jews (the name that was given to the Southern tribes of Judah, including Benjamin and the Levites) and the dispersed _____ of Israel. Matthew 15:24

14. In John 8:56, Yeshua now makes a claim that he is older than _____and that _____ saw him, which would have been over 1800 years before that. Go back to Genesis 22:14-18. God revealed to Abraham that through his obedience all _____would be_____. This was not focusing upon physical blessing, but upon spiritual blessing (the Messiah).

15. Read John 10. Yeshua now refers to himself as a _____ that is taking care of his _____, which is in contrast to the _____ or robber, who comes in and does not _____ about the sheep. See Psalm 23, written by King David.

- Once again, his words cause division and some ask, "Can a demon open the eyes of the _____?" 10:19-21

- Again, his miracles come back because the actions, not just the words, will hold true of a prophet like unto Moses (Deuteronomy 18:15). They know the Messiah will be greater than Moses, whom they thought was the greatest prophet.

- In Matthew 10:34, it is clear that Yeshua came to bring a _____. This is the same word used of the _____ of God in Hebrews 4:12. This is the Word of truth, which often brings division. Yeshua is the walking Word of God, therefore he is truth- John 1:1.

16. Read John 11. Mary and Martha are sisters and followers of Yeshua. Their brother _____ is dying and they send for him to come and heal him. After hearing the news, he waits _____ more days to go see Lazarus.

- When he arrives, Martha rushes out to see him. Yeshua says, your brother will rise again, and Martha says, "I know that he will rise again in the resurrection on the last day. Jesus says, "I am the _____ and the _____. Whoever believes in me, though he die, yet shall he live and everyone who lives and believes in me shall never die."

- He gets there and Lazarus has been dead for _____ days and then Yeshua says, "Lazarus come out. The man who was _____ came out." Yeshua not only has power to bring life, he has power over death.

  ➢ **Extreme Thought**: **Are you afraid to die?** I know this is a very direct question, but death is one of those things you can count on. Everyone who is born will eventually die. However, if you are a disciple of Jesus Christ, you may die physically but you can live eternally with him in your resurrected body. Does that make you feel better? This is a resurrected body that does not sweat, does not get broken bones and does not get tired, among other amazing blessings. I love basketball and I am hoping there will be basketball so I can dunk. I never could dunk here, so that would be cool. How about you? Some of you may think I am being a little strange or silly in approaching death, but these are real life and eternal issues that we often are too busy to actually think about, so maybe some humor will get you to think about it.

17. Jesus lived to die so that we may live. From John 12 until the end of John, you will see this unfold. In 12:1-14, Mary uses oils to _____ Jesus.

- Anointing was for a king and/or for preparation for _____. Was it for both? John 12:2-7, 19:40
- Yeshua is a king, but he will not complete that role as king on earth until his second coming.
- Read 12:13-15. What prophecy does he fulfill from Zechariah 9:9.

18. In John 13, Yeshua washes the _____ of his 12 apostles. He is God revealed in the flesh as the Son and yet he humbles himself to wash their _____.

- He was their rabbi (teacher) and he did this to set an example for them. 13:15-16.
- He now prophesies in 13:18 that one of the 12 will betray him. What is the sign? 13:26

19. Just as the crowds and Pharisees did not understand when he said, "Where I am going you will not find me," his 12 disciples did not understand as well. Jesus then says in John 14:6, "I am the _____, the _____, and the _____. No one comes to the Father except through me."

- Put another way, he is saying that I am everything that matters in life and for all eternity because I am one with my Father. If you do not follow me, you cannot see the Father and thus you cannot have His salvation.
- At the end of Exodus when the tabernacle is complete, but the people were forbidden to come except in one way. There was only one way to enter the tabernacle to come to God. Yeshua was that gate in Exodus and Leviticus and in John 10:7-9. Know that everything in scripture has meaning and it fits together like a beautiful puzzle. We serve a mighty and incredible God.

20. Read John 14:15-24 and write down how you know that you love Yeshua, that you love God. How many times does he say it?

21. In John 14:25- chapter 17, Yeshua is closer than ever and he knows he must finish preparing his apostles for the time of his departure.

- ✓ He says he will send them the _____ _____. You learned earlier that he is a helper and comforter. In 16:7-11, he tells them three specific things the Holy Spirit will do. He will convict the world about _____, _____ and _____.

- ✓ He continually says that he will do as the Father commands, thus He will do the Father's will.
- ✓ He reminds them _____ (how many) times in chapter 15, that his disciples bear much _____ (walk in righteousness). Genesis 1:28.
- ✓ He tells them that they are his _____, if they obey his commands. 15:12-14 (also see Isaiah 41:8, James 4:4).

  - ➤ **Definitive Idea:** The word "friend" used here is not the same as how you usually think of a friend. This is a relationship by faith (obedience). Yeshua knew that they truly loved Him as a friend if they walked in obedience to the commands of God because to do anything else would be in opposition of Yeshua's very being, the Word of God. Would your friends be there for you and support your love for the word of God?

This is not about the "Hey, what are you doing on Saturday night friend" or the "I text them sometimes friend." This is the close friend that you would do anything for no matter what it cost you and they reciprocate this. This friendship is like family. A true friend means commitment and action just as Yeshua talks about here. How many friends do you really have or are all your friends just on a superficial level? Do any of them help you draw closer to God or keep you accountable? I have said for years that a true believer without accountability could be in a very dangerous place. Who are you accountable to in your daily walk before God?

✓ He is preparing them in 15:18-25 for what is to come. Their task of continuing to preach the gospel will not be easy after he leaves.
✓ What are Yeshua's last words of comfort in this section (16:33)?

22. In John 17, this is the longest recorded prayer from Yeshua in the Bible.

- Yeshua does not pray the way many of us pray. In 17:14-15, he prays that trouble will come and give them the strength to get through it. We often pray that God will just give us no trouble or give us our material wants. How do you pray; be honest?

  ➤ How would you grow in your faith if you were never tested? This has come up some in previous lessons.

- John 17:17 says that the Word of _____ is truth.

  ➤ You live in a world that says there is no absolute truth. If there is no truth, then why take any tests? If there is no truth, then who decides what is truth? What if your truth clashes with my truth, then how do we settle it?

  ➤ **Truth defined** (Emet in Hebrew)- Psalm 119:142 says that the Law (Torah) of God is truth. That which is firm, faithful, established, trustworthy or that which is true. It is a picture of the "opening of a seed" which begins by forming the roots. .[23] The roots make for a strong, firm foundation. God is the only one that fits this description, thus we can trust that what He does is truth. He and His laws are the foundation of all things

  ➤ Did you know that Yeshua prayed for you specifically in John 17:20? See, it is no accident, coincidence or luck that you are a disciple of Yeshua. There is no such think as luck or coincidences with God. He knows all. If you ever have days when you get down or feel like you have no purpose, remember that Yeshua the Messiah prayed for you and still intercedes for you to the Father everyday. Be encouraged!

23. There is an important event that John does not mention in detail and that is the Passover meal (some refer to as the Last Supper). On God's calendar, the 24-hour period of a day begins at 6:00 P.M (see Genesis 1), so Yeshua is having the Passover meal after 6:00 P.M. the beginning of the day in which He is crucified. Matthew 26:17-29

24. Who comes to betray Yeshua and what does Peter do? 18:5-11

25. Peter denies Yeshua how many times? 18:15-27

26. All of this is happening on the appointed time of _____. Is this the way to obey the appointed time of the Passover? John 18:28.

27. Yeshua is brought before many people to decide if he is guilty of a crime.

    ✓ He goes before the high priests, _____ and _____.
       John 18:19-24
    ✓ He goes before _____, the governor of Rome. Luke 23:1-5
    ✓ He goes before king _____, ruler of Galilee. Luke 23:6
    ✓ He goes back to Pilate and Pilate flogged (beat) him. John 19:1-3
    ✓ The crowd, including many Jewish leaders, yells that he should be crucified because they say he is guilty of breaking God's law of blasphemy. John 19:12-16, Luke 22:70.

28. Yeshua's crucifixion and Psalm 22. Please read it to see the other prophecies come true.

    ✓ Yeshua quotes and fulfills Psalm 22:1 which says "My God my God, why have _____ forsaken me? Psalm 22:1

    ✓ Yeshua quotes and fulfills Psalm 22:31 "It is _____" in John 19:30.

    • Crucifixion was death by suffocation and/or blood loss. Three nails are used—1 through each wrist and 1 through the two feet). The victim was stretched out so far that he had to pull himself up to get air, thus tearing at his skin and bones, in order to do so. Eventually the muscles would give out and thus the victim could not push up anymore to get air, which would result in death. In some cases, and I believe it to be true of Y'shua, that he died from blood loss before the suffocation. The beating he took before even getting to the cross leads me to believe that this was the case for him. Regardless of how crucifixion killed him, he was the one that gave up His life. He was in control. Archeology and historical writings have confirmed the reality of crucifixion.

29. Details of Yeshua's death.

    ✓ He is flogged
    ✓ He has most, if not all of his clothes torn off to shame him, and then they draw lots to see who would get them.
    ✓ He has a crown of large thorns pushed into his head.
    ✓ He is given a purple cloak of royalty as a way to mock him.
    ✓ He is also spit upon which was considered one of the most shameful things someone could do to you.

✓ He is forced to bear some of the weight of the wooden cross as he walks to an impending death.
✓ Then he has the nails driven through his hands and feet.
✓ While the soldiers were waiting for him to die, they also scoff at him.
✓ One of the prisoners next to him also begins to scoff at him.
✓ As if this is not enough shame and humiliation, a soldier stabs him in the side with a sword after he is dead.

➢ If you have not thought much about the crucifixion lately, think about it now. God the Father sent His only Son and the Son willingly came as a baby to grow up and die as a man in horrible fashion, by the very people He created. He did this for your sins and mine. **If anything seems tough today, tomorrow, next week or next year, go back and re-read this. Your perspective on life will change. If you would like the visual of this event, The Passion of the Christ is the closest example of what He would have gone through.**

30. There are two great points concerning authority when you look at what happened about 2000 years ago.

✓ In John 19:12, Jesus answered Pilate, "You would have no _____ over me at all unless it had been given you from _____. Therefore he who delivered me over to you has the greater sin."

✓ In John 19:30, "When Jesus had finished the sour wine, he said, "It is _____," or all is accomplished and he bowed his head and gave up his spirit."

➢ What do you notice about these two verses concerning who was in control?

31. Yeshua is buried in a tomb that no one had ever been buried in before. John 19:41, Isaiah 59:3

• Who helped take care of the body of Yeshua? 19:38-39

➢ To remind you of how people can really get things backward morally, they crucified a man without real proof secretly in the night, but then they are so concerned about keeping the Sabbath day holy (19:31, 42). Remember that God asks us to obey all of his holy commands that are applicable for us today, not just the ones we like or the ones that are easy.

A. Memory Verse: John 14:6 and 14:15. I know it is 2 verses, but they are short. Remember introduction about ideas to memorize scripture.

B. Six questions to ask while thinking back through the text.

1. Who did Yeshua pray for in John 17:20?

2. What was Yeshua's first miracle?

3. When does Peter begin to weep?

4. Where was Yeshua found the night he was betrayed?

5. Why were the apostles afraid?

6. How did Yeshua react to his betrayal?

C. Application How does this biblical truth affect how I live my life each day? Does this explain what you see in the news each day or what you see in your family and friends?

D. Journal and prayer time. Is there a sin you need to confess? As you do this, ask God to help you live according to what you just studied. Praise God that Yeshua came, was born in a miraculous way, lived sinless and died for me and everyone else who will receive this gift!

Lesson 21: Messiah Dies: What Happens Next? (Book of Acts)

When you finished the last lesson, Yeshua (Jesus) suffered a horrible death on the cross and he fulfilled all the prophecies about his first return and then he says, "It is finished." You may be asking yourself what happened to Judas, who turned him in? Read Matthew 27 for details of his death. The Bible has some pretty exciting history. Some of your family or friends may think the Bible is boring or it does not relate to their lives in the 21st century, but you can tell them some awesome truths and get them excited about the truths of God and His free gift of eternal life. One of your memory verses for last week was John 14:15. You cannot obey the commandments completely if you do not know them. Being a student of the Word will do just that so you may love God through Jesus as never before. Okay, do not forget where you are in your studies. Yeshua is in the grave so what happens next? Did you read ahead? I am going to keep you in suspense a little longer. There is one more thing about the life of Jesus that ties into the next event that must be mentioned and it also ties many other things together. Let's go!

1. The last week of Yeshua's life is a beautiful fulfillment of foreshadowed events from Exodus 12 and other scriptures, but I will focus on Exodus 12 now. You have already seen some to this point. Let's make the timeline more complete and then move to the next event after the grave.

2. Yeshua is the High priest after the order of Melchizedek and the Passover Lamb (1 Corinthians 5:7) that takes away the sins of the world. What does this mean and how do the appointed times play into these events? Refer back to Lesson 8 #10 in Exodus 12 and Lesson 10 #6 in Leviticus 23.

- ✓ 1st of Aviv- New Beginnings. God rescued His people in Exodus 12 and 2 Corinthians 5:17, says that when you are in Christ, you are a new creation. There is something new and wonderful that happens. You have been rescued; a new beginning.
- ✓ 10th of Aviv- Passover Lamb was chosen. Yeshua rode into Jerusalem on a donkey as the chosen one to deliver the people (Messiah or Christ).
- ✓ 10th-13th of Aviv- Passover lamb is inspected for spot or blemish to see if it is worthy to offer up as a pleasing sacrifice to the LORD. Yeshua was inspected for spot or blemish to see if He was worthy to be the Great High priest to offer the sacrifice to God and the Prophet that is superior to Moses (Deuteronomy 13 and 18). Was he the spotless lamb, the Messiah?
- ✓ 14th of Aviv- Passover Lamb is slaughtered on Passover, between the eves or twilight (between 3 pm and before 6 pm to avoid doing this on the High Sabbath). Yeshua is also killed at this time to continue in His fulfillment of prophecy and further exclaim that He is the Messiah, the Lamb that takes away the sins of the world. He is the perfect High Priest, after the order of Melchizedek and His personal sacrifice would only need to be offered once as a perfect, divine sacrifice (Genesis 14:18, Hebrews 5:10, 7:11-15). Y'shua is buried before the High Sabbath on this day.
- ✓ 15th of Aviv- Feast of Unleavened Bread begins and everyone cleaned out the leaven in their houses to represent the removal of sins so they may be righteous (clean) before the

LORD. Yeshua removed all of your sins so you may be justified (declared righteous or clean) before the LORD).

✓ 17ᵗʰ of Aviv- First fruits (choicest, best) is the day Yeshua is resurrected. He is our first fruit as we are called first fruits. 1 Corinthians 15:20-23, Romans 11:16, James 1:18.

There is some debate on these dates, but as I have studied, either Yeshua died on Wednesday afternoon or Thursday afternoon. I cannot make the Friday afternoon idea work except in this way—the short time before sunset counts as a day, Shabbat is a day and then Sunday is on the third day. If he died on Friday, then he rose on the second day. There are different scriptures that talk about on the third day or after the third day, so that would make it either Wednesday or Thursday if I count full days instead of partial days. I believe personally that Yeshua died on Wednesday afternoon, which means three full days would have him rising on the Lord's day, Shabbat. Regardless, the important point to remember is His fulfillment of prophecy in the appointed times, and the fact that He did rise from the dead just as all believers will do one day. This is why the remembrance and celebration of the appointed times from Leviticus 23 is so important. They speak of our great Messiah Yeshua. See Lesson 10 #7 to connect these important dates, and why it matters.

3. On the _____ day of Jesus being in the grave (Matt. 26:61, 27:40, 63, John 2:20), Mary Magdalene came to the tomb while it was still _____and then went to get John and Peter. John 20:1

- The Messiah not only came and died, but He lives. He is resurrected (rose from the dead) so He has power over life and death. He was resurrected on Feast of First fruits.
  ➤ How many of the appointed times did Yeshua fulfill (see Leviticus 23) while on earth the first time?
- _____ said his body was missing and she went to tell the others. 2:5-8
- Did the disciples understand what had happened? 2:9-10

- Who does Yeshua appear to first after his resurrection?

  ➤ How important is the resurrection of Jesus to your faith?   1 Corinthians 15:12-17. Without it you have no hope.

  ✓ If no resurrection of the dead, then not even _____ has been raised.

  ✓ If no resurrection, then _____ of the Messiah is in vain.

  ✓ If no resurrection, then we call _____ a liar.

✓ If no resurrection, your faith is _____ and you are still dead in your

_____.

4. What are Yeshua's disciples doing at this point? 20:19

- How does Yeshua get to where they are staying? (If you are a disciple of Yeshua, you will later have a resurrected body and do these same things) 20:19, 26

  ➢ I know that some of you, especially the guys, love superheroes and have asked each other that classic question, "What super power would you have if you could have just one?" Would you like all of them? But if you want to fight villains and criminals with your powers, I have some good news and some bad news. The good news is there will be no villains and the bad news is there will be no villains. There are no bad guys at the very end when Yeshua has defeated them all, including the first bad guy ever, Satan- (Revelation 20:7-10).

- The disciples receive the Holy Spirit and are given authority to _____ people of their sins. 20:22

- Did Yeshua appear to the remaining 11 apostles and who was missing?" Read 20:24-29

- Yeshua appears to _____to help him with his lack of faith. Faith is not about sight, but about what and who you cannot see. It is not about observing, but about doing (action or obedience). It is a focus on God and His abilities and truth, not about your own abilities. See Lesson 5 #7.

5. As I stated at the beginning of lesson 19 and now you see in John 20:31, John wrote his gospel to proclaim that the *Messiah* has come and his name is Yeshua, the _____ that means _____. And if you will believe in His name, you will be part of Him (salvation). Importance of a name- (Lesson 8 #5).

6. Now what are the apostles doing? They have been given the Holy Spirit and great responsibility to forgive people their sins or not to forgive their sins, and they are going _____. Did they get their mission yet? John 21:1-11, Matthew 4:19, Jeremiah 16:16.

7. A disciple of Yeshua means many things, as you have learned. Now see what else it means.

- Being Yeshua's disciple could mean _____. John 21:18-19
- Being Yeshua's disciples means you are to go and make disciples also. What are the details of this statement found in Matthew 28:16-20?

- Being Jesus' disciple means that you have been taught by the best disciple-maker ever. So much more could be learned, but it was never written down. 21:25.

BOOK OF ACTS

8. In Acts 1:6, you can see that the apostles are still trying to understand exactly what is going on with the Messiah. He fulfilled the offices of prophet and priest, but He will not fulfill the office of king until His 2nd return. He is King of Kings, but will not show us just yet.

9. Jesus then ascends back to the Heavenly Kingdom right before their _____.

10. Peter realizes that it is time to go and make more disciples, so it is time to replace

_____. They draw lots and it fell upon _____. Acts 1:23-26

11. Read Acts 2:1. Most Bibles will say, "When the day of Pentecost arrived.." Literally, it would say, "When the fiftieth day arrived." The question that naturally arises is fiftieth day after what?

- Read Exodus 12:2 again. Their calendars were set by this day, so this was the appointed time of Shavuot (Feast of Weeks). Leviticus 23:15-22. What were they celebrating by remembering this appointed time?

- What similar event happened in Exodus 19? List the similarities between Exodus 19:16-20 and Acts 2:1-3? (Check multiple translations to help you with this comparison).

- God created man and walked with him in the Garden of Eden. God always wanted to be close to man, but sin separated this relationship. In Exodus 19 and 20:18-19, you again see God wanting to be close to his people but the people did not receive Him and thus He did not come near to have this special relationship.

- Now in Acts, you see God coming again to be near His people, the Jews (from Judah) and the lost sheep of _____ (Acts 2:5, 36). This is the time that God will come near and the Holy Spirit will dwell in them permanently.

  ➢ **Extreme Thought:** God still cannot dwell with sin, thus whenever you sin intentionally, your relationship has been severed and true repentance is necessary to restore that relationship. I use the word "intentionally" because we are all part of a sinful world and thus infected with the sin around us and in us. In other words, you do not have the ability to be sinless (1 John 1:10, Romans 3:10-12). The key is to not sin intentionally and when you realize your sins, intentional or unintentional, you repent and make it right. (See Lesson 11 #1).

12. Peter begins to preach in Acts 2:14-41, and he is quoting the OT (Tanakh) several times and the people realize that Yeshua was the Messiah that they had longed for. They _____ and are baptized. Baptism is not necessary for salvation but is an outward sign of what is happening in your heart. Although it is not necessary for salvation, it is an act that accompanies salvation from your obedience so to choose to not do this in is in direct disobedience to God's commands. Remember that you have come into covenant with the King of the Universe, your Creator. Baptism is a picture of the death to your old self and then being raised as a new creation. Throughout history, the Jews would perform a baptism (mikveh) before coming to worship as a reminder that they could only approach God with _____ hands and a _____ heart (Psalm 24).

  ❖ **Definitive Idea: Baptism-** If you have not been baptized, I want to encourage you to be obedient to this as soon as possible. Baptism is a picture of a death, burial and resurrection. You have died to your old state of being lost outside of Christ, you are buried and then you rise out of the water in new life (Acts 2:38). In the past and in many countries still today, baptisms took place in rivers and seas. This meant that you could not always do this without others knowing what you are doing. By doing this, you are making a declaration of whose side you are on. In other words, you could not hide if you were a follower of Yeshua. When you do this, you declare to the world that you follow Yeshua the Messiah. There will be no more guessing from those that know you that you have made an eternal decision for life.

13. Who initiates our salvation? Acts 2:39, John 5:21

14. What is the first miracle performed by the apostles since Yeshua has left? 3:1-8

- Did they take credit for the healing? 3:12-14

15. Peter preaches again and how many were saved? Acts 2:41, 4:4

16. The Jewish leaders question Peter and John about their actions.

- Do they change their message or are they true to the gospel of Yeshua?
- In Acts 4:12, they proclaim that "salvation is in no one else, for there is no other _____ under heaven given among men by which we must be saved."
- The Jewish leaders realize that this boldness is coming from ordinary men and then recognize that Peter and John had been with _____. 4:13
- In Acts 4:19, Peter and John know that they must obey God over man.
  - How about your journey so far? Would your family and/or people at school and work, be able to tell you have been with Yeshua (salvation)? Are you walking in holiness (set apart) as I have explained in earlier lessons? <u>What is your struggle?</u>

  - To obey God over man does not mean that you ignore laws of our state and our country. Here are some examples of things that you may have to decide in the future, whether you will obey God or man. **I want you to discuss these with your peers and/or your discipleship group leader**. You do have accountability in your walk with God, correct? You thought I was going to drop this idea of accountability, but it is too important (Lesson 20 #21).

- ✓ Abortion is legal but does that make it right?
- ✓ Divorce is legal but does that make it right?
- ✓ Sex before marriage is legal but does that make it right?
- ✓ Co-ed dorms and/or co-ed bathrooms are legal in some colleges, but does that mean you need to go to that college?
- ✓ Downloading some songs and movies without paying for them is illegal. Will you stop doing what is illegal today?
- ✓ Teaching that God is the creator of all things is illegal in many schools. If you are a student, will you ask why this is not taught? If you are a teacher, will you teach it?
- ✓ Teaching that homosexuality is normal and should be accepted in our schools is becoming mandatory in many schools. Will you take a peaceful and loving stance against this? Will you teach this?

✓ Teaching that teens are going to have sex anyway, so we should just give them condoms. Will you take the condoms? Will you teach this?

✓ Teaching that Islam is a religion of peace and some schools are requiring students to practice certain Muslim beliefs, including saying the Islamic prayer for salvation. Will you participate? Will you teach this?

Remember that compromise and doing nothing is just like teaching it, even if you are not a teacher! Your actions are displaying what you believe. Circle 3 areas where you struggle to stand up for truth or where you may not know much about the topic. You may find a cause to fight for in this list or you may decide you want to stop going to public school?

17. When you read Acts chapter 4, you see that God's people are unselfish and loving. Now you get to a little different story in Acts 5.

- Did God require that they give all the money for the sell of the land?
- They were prideful and tried to show off how holy they were. Who did they lie to (more than one)? 5:1-4 You see 2 of the 3 centers of identity of the one true God.

➢ Do not try to show off to God. He is not impressed nor can you hide anything from Him anyway. Just come with a humble and selfless heart each day. How is your pride this week? James 4:4

18. Stephen, a disciple of Yeshua, speaks with boldness and truth. He is speaking to people from the 12 tribes of Israel. As they were listening to him, they do not like what he is saying. What happens in 7:54-60?

19. Who is approving of the execution of Stephen? 8:1-3

20. What was Saul's purpose as he travels in 9:1-2?

- Who appears to him in 9:3-5?
- What physically happens to him in 9:7-8
- What does the Lord say will happen to Saul in 9:15-16?
- How long does Saul leave before he returns to proclaim the gospel (many believe he was training as a disciple during this time)? Galatians 1:17-19

A. Memory Verse: Acts 4:12- I like the NIV Bible on this one.

B. Six questions to ask while thinking back through the text.

1. Who was resurrected on the third day?

2. What did the apostles see inside the tomb?

3. When did Mary arrive at the tomb?

4. Where did Yeshua appear to his apostles after his resurrection?

5. Why were the apostles there?

6. How did Yeshua get into the room?

C. **Application** How does this biblical truth affect me each day?

D. **Journal and prayer time**. Is there a sin you need to confess? As you do this, ask God to help you live according to what you have studied. Is there a praise for your Creator today?

Lesson 22: Jews, Greeks and Gentiles—Same God, Same Salvation, Same Law
(Acts and Galatians)

I have tried not to give you too much historical context, as it can take much explanation, but I hope I have given you enough where it is necessary. Beginning in Acts 10 and throughout the apostolic writings (remainder of the NT), you need to understand what is happening. The assembly (same word that is translated as church in English) that began in Exodus, was kept alive by a remnant, has now just expanded by 8,000 people, will soon expand even more.

The major difference is that the assembly that has continued (through exile and restoration), from Exodus has been the Jews (tribe of Judah, tribe of Benjamin and some of the Levites). Now the gospel will go to the 10 dispersed tribes that are living like Greeks or those that do not know the Torah (teachings of God), for they have been assimilated into the culture. In other words, they do not look like God's chosen people anymore, but they are. The Jews knew that the Samaritans were half-Jewish or a mix between one of the tribes and a pagan nation, but they would not even eat with them or walk on the same side of the street as them. Therefore, many issues will arise as the apostles have to figure out how to get the Jews and the Greeks (10 scattered tribes of Israel) and the Gentiles or sojourners from other nations to get along as an assembly of God's people. Refer back to Lesson 8 #11. The Jews know the Torah and the God they serve, and are supposed to know how to live and the others have forgotten or never knew. I prefer the word "assembly" over "church" because people often think of church as a building or only when people meet at a building that says "church" on it. The word "assembly" is consistent throughout Scripture, the concept of "church" is not.

Go back to Lesson 17 #4 where Josiah reads the Torah and realizes their disobedience. This is similar in that they have also forgotten the heart of Torah, which is life and truth from the heart of God. This is the historical context so that you will think about it this way while studying it. Your main characters will be Peter, James and Saul (Paul). It is time to follow their journeys during this exciting time of the growth of God's assembly (church). Are you ready to do some travelling? Check out these maps to understand the geography better (visual can help sometimes). *http://www.ccel.org/bible/phillips/CN092MAPS1.htm*

1. In Acts 10:1-10, _____ and _____ both receive a vision from God.

- Cornelius is to send for Peter to come to his _____. 10:19-22
- Peter sees reptiles and birds and the Lord tells him to eat and he says, "By no means, Lord; for I have never _____ anything that is common or unclean. Leviticus 11 and Deuteronomy 14 are about animals that are to be eaten and those that are not. How many times did God have to show Peter so that He would understand what He was to do? What does this tell us about Peter's obedience to God's laws about what he should eat?

- Was God's primary purpose here to talk to Peter about eating clean or unclean animals or was God using something that Peter would relate to in order to help him understand his mission to go to those "out of covenant" and bring them into covenant?

  - Could you use this Scripture to teach people today that God does not have current teachings about what we eat; about what He defines as food? If this is true, then who determines what we should eat and how is this determined? Psalm 119:33-40, Proverbs 14:12

2. Who can receive God's salvation? 10:35, 11:17-18

3. Peter goes to visit the assembly in Antioch and there the _____ of Jesus Christ are first called _____ 11:26

  - Did the fact that they were now called Christians or followers of the Christ change how they were to live? Did they have the same Torah (teachings of God) to follow or were there now new teachings to follow?

  - The only difference is instead of looking forward to the coming _____, they could now proclaim that He came and rose on or after the _____ day 10:39-41

4. What miracle happens to Peter in Acts chapter 12?

5. _____ and Barnabbas are going to the mission field (often referred to as Saul's 1st missionary journey) and begins with _____ of Pisidia in 13:1-3, 14 (approximately 44 A.D).

- What was the purpose of these missionary journeys? Matthew 28:16-20, Mark 16:15, Acts 1:8, 20:24

- What did they participate in that happened every Sabbath and still happens today in Jerusalem and many other assemblies throughout the world? 13:15

- Saul proclaims that Yeshua (Jesus) was the Messiah and he quotes 4 times from where in 13:33-41?

- What happens on the next Sabbath in 13:44-48 and were more saved?

- What happens to Saul and Barnabbas in 13:50-51 and how do they respond? Read Matthew 10:14

- They now go to Iconium, then Lystra and Derbe. 13:51, 14:6. Why did they leave Iconium? 14:1-5

- Saul and Barnabbas go from being _____ as gods to Saul being _____ and dragged out of the city by some of the Jews. 14:8-19

- They end up in Antioch and stay there just a few days. T or F
- Saul's first missionary ends at Antioch and then they go to _____ in order to settle an issue that has arisen among the assembly of believers. 15:1-2

6. Chapter 15 is usually referred to as the Jerusalem Council. They are meeting to discuss circumcision and salvation and to understand how they can teach and fellowship with the new believers, who have little or no understanding of Torah.

- Some Jews were trying to say that circumcision was necessary for _____. Peter says that salvation will come through _____, not works. 5:8-11

- What commandments should the believers obey as they are beginning their new lives, which is a path of righteousness in Christ? (Answer questions below)

  - ✓ To abstain from things polluted by _____ (food sacrificed to idols), Exodus 20:3-5, 34:15-16, Leviticus 10:4, 26:1
  - ✓ Abstain from _____ immorality, Leviticus 18, Exodus 20:14, 32:6, 1 Corinthians 6:18, 2 Timothy 2:22
  - ✓ Abstain from what has been _____ (the issue of blood again and unclean animals)
  - ✓ Abstain from eating _____. Genesis 9:4, Leviticus 17:10-16, Deuteronomy 12:23

  - ➢ Why are only these four things given as requirements to the non-Jews that know the Messiah? Is this all they must obey, but the Jews that know the Messiah have to obey all commandments? Does this sound right? Also read Acts 15:29, 21:25 to understand when they would learn later.

➤ Where do 3 of these 4 commandments come from? Exodus 20, Deuteronomy 10. So the other 7 listed in these verses are now optional?

- What is the main point they are trying to show these new believers? (Hint: You cannot serve both God and _____).
- Would they eventually learn more and obey more? The answer is found in Acts 15:21, where each _____ the Word of God is read and discussed. Same thing today for you as you go to church and learn more each week. God holds us responsible for what we know as we grow in Him. In other words, once we are in the Kingdom, we are to walk in obedience, but we don't know everything yet. Remember God is gracious when we fail in ignorance and when we fail in knowledge.

7. Saul (Paul's) 2nd missionary journey begins in Acts 16 and this time his partner is Silas. They go through several cities and end up in Philippi, a Roman colony. In English we say Saul or Paul; Shaul in Hebrew and Paulos in Greek. It was not uncommon to have multiple names and it might have been more advantageous for him to go by his Greek name considering his past. The main point is that when Shaul encountered the Messiah on the road to Damascus, he did not convert from following God's commands, but instead still lived according to the Torah (God's commands) but now believed that Yeshua was the Messiah. Matthew 5:17-20.

- Paul and Silas are beaten and thrown into prison for what reason? 16:16-24

- What are they doing in prison? 16:25

- Acts 16:26 says, "And suddenly there was a great _____, so that the foundations of the prison were shaken. And immediately all the _____ were opened, and everyone's bonds were unfastened."

- What was the prison guard about to do in 16:27 and why? What happens instead in verses 28-34?

- What news made the Roman leaders afraid? 16:37-40

8. Saul (Paul) and Silas now travel to Thessalonica. 17:1-4

- How long did they stay there and what were they doing?

- Things go much smoother for Saul in Thessalonica (17:5-8). T or F
- Now they go to Berea (17:10) and they notice something special about the people there, "they received the word with all eagerness, _____ the Scriptures daily to see if these things were so."
  - ➢ I pray that as you grow in your knowledge of the Word and thus in your relationship with God, you will be just like the Bereans. Keep reading and studying the Word each day of each year so that you may know true and false teachings just like the Bereans.
- Paul and Silas now go to Athens where the people only serve one God. T or F

9. Saul now goes to Corinth in Acts 18 and he stays there for 18 weeks. T or F

1 and 2 THESSALONIANS

- Many scholars believe that Paul wrote **1 and 2 Thessalonians** during this time period (about AD 50-51). Read these two short letters (30 minutes or less).

- **1 and 2 Thessalonians**, as with most letters from Paul or other apostles, are in response to letters that they received. These letters have been lost and so we can only get a good idea of what they say by the response that is given. Paul is writing to encourage them in their beliefs and to help them deal with some leaders who are spreading false teachings in order to lead some people astray. At the conclusion of 1 Thessalonians, Paul tells them to encourage one another, abstain from evil and to test everything against what is true. He wants them to know truth so they will not be led astray. In 2 Thessalonians, these false teachers were telling the people they had missed the second coming of Yeshua the Messiah. He assures them that there are signs to look for and Yeshua will not come without these warning signs. These are the same signs we are to look for today and as believers, we will not be surprised, as if Yeshua's coming is like a thief in the night. Only unbelievers will be surprised.

  He ends by encouraging them to keep walking in righteousness despite the current persecution. I have mentioned how important context is and here is another one of those places. Just because a teaching is popular, does not necessarily mean it is true. Let the scriptures teach you truth. In 1 Thessalonians 4:13-17, which is one of the core passages used for the "pre-tribulation rapture" concept in which no believer will suffer for their faith, but be taken up to the clouds and leave the earth before the tribulation. Without getting into a full teaching on this subject, the context from history is that they were being persecuted. Is it not ironic that a core passage used to push a certain eschatological idea of no persecution is right in the middle of a book written during a time of immense persecution? Does Emperor Nero ring a bell? Check out some of his persecutions.

GALATIANS

10. Paul ends his 2nd missionary journey in Antioch and begins his 3rd missionary journey in Galatia (Acts 18:22-28) and then to Ephesus, where he spends 3 years (20:31). It will take you about 30 minutes to read.

- Paul probably wrote Galatians during this time (about 53 AD).
- Galatians is a letter from the apostle Paul to a church that is dealing with Judaizers who were teaching a false gospel (1:6, 2:4). These are Jewish men who were telling the non-Jews that salvation came through obeying the laws of God. Paul is warning them against this teaching and correctly teaches them that obeying the law is not for salvation, but it reveals your obedience to God in your salvation through His grace. The law was not for entering into salvation (into the Kingdom of God), because no one can perfectly obey the perfect and holy laws of God except for Yeshua. To attempt to obey the law for entering salvation would bring a curse upon you and your inability as a sinner. The law was not the curse, but your sins are the curse and thus your efforts to personally achieve salvation will always bring a curse to you, the sinner. Obedience to the laws of God is to be pursued on your first day when entering the Kingdom of the King of the Universe and His vassal King Yeshua until the last day of your life. Many of them you are already obeying and you do not even realize.

- In Galatians 3:7-9, "And the Scripture, _____ that God would justify the non-Jews by faith, preached the gospel beforehand to Abraham saying, in you shall all the_____ be blessed (Genesis 12:3, 22:18). So then those who are of faith are blessed along with Abraham, the man of faith." God knows the past, the present and the future. The same gospel of salvation by grace through faith, coming with a repentant heart, will always be the gospel message. Of course, the grace is from God, our faith rests upon God and God is holy so we can only come in repentance. It is always about God and His Son Yeshua (salvation) and we get to participate in it.

- Galatians 4:16 refers to Genesis 22:18. The offspring or _____ is Yeshua the Messiah or Jesus the Christ. Paul goes on to say that the law was officially given after the promise or covenant. God's covenant is still the same covenant in how man is saved and by whom He is saved. Paul goes on to explain in 4:21 that the _____ is not contrary to the promises of God. The law has a purpose but that purpose is not to enter the first day in God's Kingdom or salvation.

  ➢ **Critical Thought**: Freedom in Christ- Being a believer is about freedom as you see in Galatians 5, but this freedom does not come without responsibility or obedience to Jesus the Christ. The term is "freedom _in_ Christ." It is not a freedom to do whatever you want whenever you want because the Messiah did not die on the cross for you to do whatever you want. This would be describing bondage or imprisonment, not freedom. This would be your version of freedom that would be living outside the boundaries of your Messiah and this would be in opposition to His ways and thus not freedom at all. If you can do whatever you want then Yeshua died for nothing and you are still under a curse for eternity. See Galatians 5:19-24.

A. Memory Verse: Galatians 2:20. (Write it out here).

B. Six questions to ask while thinking back through the text.

1. Who was not with Jesus but counted as an apostle?

2. What was the main purpose of the vision in Acts 10?

3. When does one have true freedom?

4. Where did Paul go while training as a disciple?

5. Why are Paul's letters written?

6. How can one be saved according to Paul?

C. **Application** How does this biblical truth affect how I live my life each day? Does this explain what you see in the news each day or what you see in your family and friends? Praise God for our inability to save ourselves and God's amazing love and grace through Yeshua in order to be saved.

D. Journal and prayer time. Is there a sin you need to confess? As you do this, ask God to help you live according to what you have studied.

Lesson 23: Paul--Apostle, Missionary, Writer and Counselor (1 and 2 Corinthians)

You will see as you walk through the book of Acts, you will frequently be introduced to the letters that Paul wrote. Paul was continually receiving letters and writing letters, which would also include his letters he wrote while in prison. Paul never stopped proclaiming the gospel of Jesus the Christ. He was doing his best to help each assembly by encouragement, great counsel (Godly wisdom) and preaching the truths of God. This zealous proclamation of the gospel, wherever he goes, gets him mocked, beaten, imprisoned, and more. Do you remember what Yeshua said to him in Acts 9:16? Go on, look it up if you have forgotten.

1. In Acts 19:21-22, Paul stays in Asia for a while and many believe that he wrote 1st and 2nd Corinthians while in Asia around 55-57 AD. In 1 Corinthians, Paul (Saul) is replying to a letter he has received concerning divisions in the church. I would like to tell you that today's church is exempt from divisions and fights, but they still exist.

- From 1 Corinthians 1:17, 2:1, 4:6-7, you can see that part of the issue was preachers or
  philosophers that spoke with great eloquence or what some may call great stage presence.
  They were bringing to doubt Paul's apostleship (authority). They knew how to say just the
  right words in just the right way. The problem is that they are leading people away from
  the true gospel with man's _____, not God's _____ (1:19-25, 3:18-21).

- These men were full of pride and wanted to be recognized for what they were doing for
  God, but actually they desired _____ from men more than from God
  (John 12:43).

- Paul makes a great statement concerning this matter from 1:12-13 and now 3:5-6, "I
  _____, Apollos _____, but God gave the _____. So neither he
  who plants nor he who waters is anything, but only _____ who gives the growth,"
  (growth of the individuals that make up each assembly).

  - ➢ **Extreme Thought: Every Moment-** In 3:10-17, Paul talks about building upon a
    foundation, which is Yeshua the Messiah (Jesus the Christ), the Word of God. Paul also
    talks about the fact that you are God's temple and it is holy; so think about how you live
    with one another. What we do in this world matters for eternity. Not everyone who is
    saved for eternity will serve God in the same way. It is because we will also be judged on
    our works within our salvation. How does this understanding of Scripture make a
    difference in how you will live your daily life?

➤ As I have stated before, when you talk about the Messiah, He is the living Word of God. Your foundation is upon the Word of God, who is the Messiah (John 1:1-2). These descriptions are distinct but are never separated. To rest upon the Word of God as your foundation is to rest upon the Messiah Yeshua. How is your time in the Word, how is your foundation standing up?

➤ In verse 16, the word "you" is in the plural, which means it is referring to the assembly (church). You are not saved to live by yourself or for yourself, but you are saved into a body of believers (1 Corinthians 12:11-16). Are you gossiping about other believers or other people? Are you trying to "one up" other people? Suggestions or prayer is one thing, but gossip is another. What can you do to change this?

➤ James 1:19 says, "Everyone should be quick to _____, slow to _____ and slow to become angry." The church does not need your help to tear it down. The world is working hard enough to do this already.

2. "All things are lawful or permissible but not all things are helpful or beneficial." This phrase is used in 6:12 and 10:23 (you will need to read a few more verses to get some context).

➤ At first glance, it seems like Paul is saying you can do whatever you want. Does this sound like what you have learned up to this point? Read Romans 6:1-11, Acts 15:19-21 and Lesson 22 #11. What do you think Paul was saying?

• Also, look at what Paul says in 1 Corinthians 10:1-9. You cannot do whatever you want to do, just as Moses and the people in the desert could not put God to the test, so do not put _____ to the test. God's people can never just do whatever they want without any thoughts or consideration for God's law (God's character). You are in covenant.

• Read 1 Corinthians 10:1-4. Who is the Rock? See Exodus 17:6, 33:21-22, Numbers 20:8.

• The LORD was not just saying to ask for water from a physical rock or to hide in a physical rock, but it is about the Rock, _____ the _____. Read John 4:13-15, 7:38.

➤ I pray you are noticing that the Bible is one book with one message of salvation from Genesis through Revelation. Yeshua (salvation) is seen throughout Scripture. When you do future discipleship studies, these things will be brought up even more, but for now, I want you to see the amazing consistency of your God. He is proclaiming truth for you to see in each page. Read the Bible expecting God to speak to you and reveal amazing things. Take them and walk in them.

2 CORINTHIANS

3. In 2 Corinthians, Paul responds to another letter by writing this letter. In chapter 1 and 2, you can see that Paul is still dealing with the issue of men that are boasting in their wisdom. He begins by focusing upon how a believer will be afflicted or suffers, and all believers are to comfort one another. (1:3-7). He is still teaching unity, not division.

➤ Do you know that following Jesus will still get you beaten, imprisoned or killed in over 50 countries in our world today? Go back to John chapter 15 and 16, specifically 16:33 and see what Jesus tells you about suffering. If someone told you that being saved will make your life easier and you will not suffer, you need to go back to him or her, and lovingly say that the Bible does not teach this. Instead, a believer in Yeshua the Messiah will go wherever He sends and do whatever is to be done, which may mean suffering. Go to **www.persecution.com** and read about those that are suffering daily for Yeshua. Lastly, read 2 Timothy 3:12 and take a moment to pray about this in your own life.

• What is Paul's amazing perspective in 2 Corinthians 4:16-18 concerning suffering?

• How can he say this in light of 2 Corinthians 11:23-30? How does he keep this perspective? Where was he when he wrote Philippians? Philippians 1:13, 21

4. Read 2 Corinthians 5:11-21

• Who do you live for?

• What happens when you are saved?

• How can you be reconciled back to God?

5. In 6:14-18, Paul gives some great counsel concerning how you should approach friendships, relationships with the opposite sex and business partnerships. There is some deeper meaning to these verses, but you can just look at it from these areas for now.

> According to Paul, name the 5 reasons you cannot just date whomever you want, be friends (see Lesson 21 #21) with whomever you want and go into business with whomever you want? Also, list the verses (OT) that Paul uses to support his wise counsel.

6. In 9:6-8, Paul talks about giving to help the assembly (church) in their efforts to minister first to one another (take care of the temple where God dwells) and to reach the community with the gospel. See Exodus 25:1-2, 35:5, 1 Corinthians 6:16-17.

> **Critical Thought: Giving-** The love of money is the root of many kinds of evil (1 Timothy 6:10). As a young person, you may be thinking, "I do not have much money." Generosity is not based on the amount, but on the condition of your heart. Are you stingy or giving? If **you** only make $5.00 a week, then make sure God gets some of this. He owns it all anyway so do not act like you are doing Him a favor by giving to Him. Instead, know that it is all His and He is just loaning it to you, until you die, to use for His glory. Giving is part of God's testing. How are you doing on this test? Malachi 3:10

A. Memory Verse: 2 Corinthians 5:17 (if you can, memorize 5:15-17; write all 3 verses here)

B. Six questions to ask while thinking back through the text.

1. Who is the Rock throughout the Bible?

2. What is happening in the Corinthian church?

3. When could suffering happen in your life?

4. Where does Paul point when it comes to growth?

5. Why will it help them if they discredit Paul?

6. How are they trying to divide?

C. Application How does this biblical truth affect how I live my life each day? Does this explain what you see in the news each day or what you see in your family and friends?

D. Journal and prayer time. Is there a sin you need to confess? As you do this, ask God to help you live according to what you have just studied. Praise God for His words that guide you daily.

Lesson 24: Paul--The Determined Preacher (Romans and Ephesians)

Paul continues on his journeys and it is under constant persecution but he preaches in prison, under arrest and anywhere there is a breathing human being. In this lesson, you will look at a few more events as Paul travels and then look briefly at the books of Romans and Ephesians. Paul writes the book of Romans according to 1 Corinthians 1:14, 15:25-26 and Romans 16:23. He writes it in Corinth shortly after his third missionary journey. Paul intends to take up a collection from other churches for the church in Jerusalem and then he wants to go to Rome. God allows this to happen, but maybe not exactly how Paul thought it might play out. While in Jerusalem, he is dragged out of the temple by some angry Jews (Acts 21). He is then able to give his testimony (Acts 9), which is always about an encounter with Jesus the Christ. Read Acts 21-22. If you took my suggestion and are reading a few pages each day, you have already read it, so just skim through it at least, to get some context.

1. Paul (Saul) is being accused of disobeying the laws of God. As you have learned, Paul could not claim to be a follower of Jesus Christ and disobey the laws of God. 21:21

- Paul is obeying the law and so he decides to do something that will prove to them that he is obeying the laws of God. He takes a Nazirite vow, along with _____ other men (21:17-24). When someone takes this vow, they will do certain things as you have learned in Lesson 14 #8. Another thing that is detailed in a Nazirite vow in Numbers 6:13-21 is to offer several different _____.

- ➤ **Critical Thought: Obedience to the Law (instructions of God)** Paul was making a couple of things clear to them. First, it is okay to still offer sacrifices because offering sacrifices was about drawing near to God, not about salvation, as discussed on pg. 31. Jesus is the sacrifice once for all, but He would not condemn someone bringing their first fruits to the temple (that was still standing) or in their daily life (Romans 12:1-2). After all, He is the first fruits (1 Corinthians 15:20 and we are to follow His examples, (2 Thessalonians 2:13, James 1:18).
  He also wants us to come before God with a pure heart and walk in continual faith and obedience to God who saved you. Next, he is reconfirming that he is not forming some new religion, but still following the same salvation given by the God of Abraham, Isaac and Jacob. He will continue to walk in obedience and sanctification. It is very similar to the idea in many churches that once you are "saved" then you do not need to obey the laws of God (or be Torah observant), but instead just let the Holy Spirit lead you. Please read John chapters 14-16 and you will see that he is preparing them for his death, resurrection and ascension back to Heaven, so He is sending the Spirit to help them walk in the commands of God. The Spirit of God cannot take someone away from the commands of God, but instead by the Spirit gives them a stronger desire to obey the laws of God (Paul teaches this same idea in Romans chapters 6-8). This makes no more sense than telling a Jew that the Messiah came and they should discontinue approaching and

worshipping God as they always have. The Jews that recognized Yeshua as the Messiah, still continued to give their first fruits to God, both physically and spiritually. I obey the laws (commands) of God as I walk out my salvation with fear and trembling. Otherwise, I make up my own idea of laws and morality. That is not freedom, but bondage to my sinful self. This is not about forming a new religion but about serving the same and only God, the God of Abraham, Isaac and Jacob through His revealed Son Yeshua.

2. In chapter 22, Paul (Saul) steps up and gives his testimony.

> **Definitive Thought: Your Testimony**- I need you to stop this lesson for about 30 minutes or more and write out what your life has been about up until today. What was your life like before you were saved by grace through faith? Write it out now. It is important to give your testimony to others when God allows, because no one can ever take away the truth of God's salvation in your life. Also, everyone has a testimony if they are saved. You were lost and now you are found, you were dead and now you are alive. Write it out on another sheet of paper. You should be able to give your testimony in 5 minutes or less. Remember that your testimony is more about God than you. In other words, do not go on and on about how bad your life was, but mention some of it, get to the gospel of how God saved you and give them the opportunity to receive the same salvation, if you feel God is leading you to share it with them that day.

ROMANS

3. As with all these letter summaries I give you, there is so much more, but you are learning enough for now.

- Romans 1:16-17. Paul is not ashamed of the _____, for it is the power of God for _____ to everyone who believes, to the Jew first and then to the Greek. Paul is using the term "Greek" to refer to the 10 scattered tribes as you learned in the gospels. Yeshua came to restore the responsibility to the 12 tribes that were called at Mt. Sinai and thus the mission is still Jews and Greeks and then all others (Gentiles) who will come into covenant salvation with God.

- Read chapters 2-3. Why is there a distinction in being a Jew (tribe of Judah, tribe of Benjamin and the Levites)? 2:19-21, 3:1-2.

- Does salvation depend upon the Jews ability or the Jews faithfulness? 3:1-4

- What is the central problem to all nations? Read 3:10-18 List at least 4 problems. See 1 Kings 8:46. Where is Paul quoting?

- Romans 3:23 says, "For all have _____ and fall short of the _____ of God."

  ➤ **Extreme Thought!** Your purpose for existing is to bring glory to God. Since all sin, then how can you do this? How can you be justified (see definition below)? Romans 3:24

  ❖ **Justified Defined** (Dikaioo in Greek and Tsadaq in Hebrew)- One who is upright or righteous is one who walks a straight path; cleansed, just or righteous. [24] You cannot be justified on your own due to your sin. Jesus justifies you and by receiving salvation you are declared righteous. Your ability to be righteous depends solely upon your connection (salvation), to the God of salvation and understanding that he emanated or revealed Himself as a person in His Son and he died for you.

4. Romans 3:25-26- these are very important verses for you to understand. God is just and righteous, so he does not need to be justified nor made righteous, but you need some help.

- God is able to justify and proclaim righteousness upon all who receive His grace and act in faith. In verse 25, God passed over _____ sins in order to show His righteousness. In other words, God has always been righteous and God has also saved in the same way, but God's grace (same grace as in Genesis 3) was not revealed yet in the form of His only Son, the Messiah.

- What does Jesus do to display God's grace for all sinners? John 1:16-17, 19:30

- In John 1:16-17, God's grace and truth were ultimately revealed. Grace and truth had already been seen, but not in walking perfection as in Jesus the Christ. You can see this grace in Romans 4:7-8, as Paul quotes Psalm 12:1-2.

- Circumcision was a sign of the covenant, but not an act to achieve salvation. When was Abraham circumcised? Romans 4:9-12. Why is the order important?

➤ **Definitive Thought: Hope-** How do you know you have can have hope? How many of your friends (it may still be you), think you can feel secure in the hope of salvation by living however you want. Paul says that through these 3 things, you will understand the hope you have. Otherwise, you will live just like the world. Think about how you are living. Paul talks about it more in 8:22-25. Name the 3 things.

5. In Romans 5:6 Paul writes, "For while we were still _____ (sinful), at the right time, Christ died for the _____." He did not die for you because you had something to offer, but you were in opposition to Him.

6. Where did sin come from and what type of gift do we get? Romans 5:12-15

➤ Does Paul talk about this free gift as if it costs you nothing or as if it cost Yeshua nothing? 6:1-4 Things that are free always come with a cost. Look back at the suffering Yeshua went through on the cross. Your salvation is not free so how should you live?

➤ Do you like encouragement? Read 8:31-39 and see that each saved person is safe in the hands of a holy and loving God. How does this encourage you?

7. Romans chapters 9-11. Read 9:1-9 right now. Paul is a Jewish Rabbi and you can feel the anguish in his voice as he begins Romans 9. He knows the amazing responsibility that the Jews have received. List their 8 privileges (responsibilities).

- Romans 9:7-13 says that all children of Abraham are spiritual children of Abraham. T or F (Also see 9:27)
- When you read 9:14-23, it is clear that God is in control of all things. T or F
- Romans 9:29 quotes Isaiah 1:9 and says that "if the LORD of hosts had not left us offspring we would have been like Sodom and become like Gomorrah." What happened to these cities? Genesis 19:23-28

8. In chapter 10:8-18, Paul proclaims the gospel and he says all can be saved.

- All can be saved, but will all be saved?

- Has God exclaimed the gospel everywhere so man is without excuse on the Day of Judgment (Ezekiel 18:23, Romans 1:18-21, 2 Corinthians 5:10)?

- Who are those that will preach the gospel? Romans 10:15-18, Psalm 19:1-4 (Paul quotes from Psalm 19:4). Is man without excuse?

9. Romans 11- Same mission, different method.

- Paul is still keeping the same mission, which is to reach the Jew first, then the Greek. Now the Gentiles (those out of covenant or salvation) will need to do their part to show the Jews their responsibility and privilege before God.
- Read 11:11-25. What are the Gentiles asked to do in Romans 11:11?

- How can they make Israel (Jews) jealous? By obeying the _____ of God, which means walking in _____. No Jew will ever listen to our claims that Yeshua (Jesus) is the Messiah unless we walk in righteousness according to God's laws. Righteousness does not mean perfection.

- God is going to graft together the Jews and the Gentiles. God wanted the Jews to be a light to the world but they were disobedient. Now the Gentiles will be grafted in.

- In 11:25-26, Paul calls this "grafting in" a mystery. Now look back to Genesis 48:19 and see the following phrase also used there-"until the fullness of the Gentiles has come in." God knew all along what was going to happen. His plan did not fail. He did not have some backup plan he had to implement because Plan A failed. Not our God. You may not be following all of this, so let me explain. God is doing something new. He is making a covenant with people that have no covenant. This is huge! Jeremiah 31:31 says that God will renew his covenant with the house of Israel and the house of Judah, so this means that if you are not from the 12 tribes, you could not be in covenant with God. Romans 11 states that if you are a non-Jew, you can be in covenant with God and be saved. YES! Same God, same salvation, same laws. **He saved you to change you.** You will not do this unless you walk in His ways (laws). Gentiles were without a covenant and thus without opportunity for salvation .The term "Gentile Christian" makes no sense, because you are declaring yourself out of covenant. Instead, when you are redeemed, you become "Israel" as Paul says in Romans 11 and Ephesians 2. As Gentiles, they did not replace the nation of Israel as "replacement theology" teaches, but you are part of Israel and thus have some of the same promises as well.

10. Read Romans 12 before going further - How will you live?

- Read Romans 12:1-2. Does Paul's speech remind you of temple talk? Offer, sacrifice, holy, etc. Today, there is no longer any temple to offer sacrifices and Yeshua came and died "once for all" _____(Hebrews 7:27, 9:28). However, God is still the same holy God and you cannot just approach any way you want. You approach in purity, humility and repentance. See Lesson 10, beginning pages about drawing near to God.

  ❖ **Extreme Thought: Living Sacrifice-** There is still a sacrifice to make, but what type is it? You are the daily sacrifice whom others see by how you live. When you live for yourself, you are bringing an unacceptable sacrifice. When you walk in righteousness and obedience, you offer an acceptable sacrifice. Romans 12:2. Write out at least 3 things that you need to do from this verse and be specific to what you struggle with.

  ➢ Read Romans 12:3. Is it about you?

  ➢ Read Romans 12:9-21. List at least 5 things and think about how you are living. This will change you and those around you if you walk in obedience.

EPHESIANS

11. This is one of my favorite books, but I can only cover a few verses. Take 30 minutes to read it before beginning.

- Ephesians 1 is about your new identity. List some adjectives that Paul uses to describe your position in Christ.

- Ephesians 2:1-10- Now that you understand how privileged you are from chapter 1, Paul describes the salvation journey from the point of what you were saved from. A gospel message is never complete without understanding your place as a sinner. Follow these verses and you will see a salvation picture. Make a chart and list before and after facts.

- Ephesians 2:12-13. Remember what you just studied in Romans 11. You now have hope; you are now in covenant and saved by God. 3:6.

- Ephesians Chapters 3 and 4- I will give you 2 questions to answer:
  ➤ What is your purpose in Christ according to Paul?

  ➤ What can you do to keep from living out of purpose?

- Ephesians 5:1-7. Who are you to imitate?

  ➤ How serious is God about sexual immorality, impurity and coveting? Has this changed from what you studied in God's Word so far?

  ➤ Does God like dirty jokes, crude comments about the opposite sex, or joking at other's expense? Your speech and thoughts should be about _____, (5:4) not about putting others down, trying to fit in, etc. Take a stand and do what is righteous. How are you doing in these areas?

- Ephesians 5:22-33- This is talking about Christ's relationship with His bride (we are the bride, his body of believers). How are we to treat one another? Same as Romans 12. It also shows how a husband and wife are to treat one another. *Marriage is the closest relationship we have to understand our relationship with God.* This is why marriage is so sacred to God and it grieves Him that the divorce rate within the church is the same as outside the church.

  - ➤ **Extreme Thought**: **MARRIAGE**- What will you do to prepare for marriage so yours will be more like the description in Ephesians 5? It takes time and work to make a great marriage. <u>Will you take the time to get true counseling before marriage?</u> This includes prayer ministry that gets to the core of lies that you have believed in life to help you to get to a maturing life of repentance and unselfishness. These sound overwhelming but so is a miserable marriage and divorce, so the choice is yours. Most people spend too much time and money preparing a wedding and forget that this is one day compared to the rest of your life. **Girls Ask Yourself 2 Questions**: <u>Will it be about the wedding or the marriage?</u> Is the man you are going to marry leading you in a way that reflects the covenant of marriage?

- Ephesians 6:1-4- "Children _____ your parents in the Lord for this is _____. Honor your _____ and _____."
  - ➤ How are you doing on this? Obedience is not what you think or feel about them from day to day. In other words, they are not perfect but you still respect and obey them. Now if they tell you to do something against God's Word, this will be tough, so what will you do? Many decisions will be tough if they do not love the Lord. Honor them. Read Acts 4:19-20

A. Memory Verse: Romans 12:2, Ephesians 6:1-2. (Write them out here).

B. Six questions to ask while thinking back through the text.

1. Who is responsible to obey the laws of God?

2. What picture is given for us to understand our relationship with God in Ephesians 5?

3. When was grace originally revealed in Scripture?

4. Where do we meet with God today?

5. Why do we ultimately exist?

6. How can one be saved outside of covenant or can they?

C. Application How does this biblical truth affect me each day?

D. Journal and prayer time. Is there a sin you need to confess? As you do this, ask God to help you live according to what you have just studied. Praise God for your position in Christ. What a privilege.

Lesson 25: The Practical Life of Faith and Suffering (James and Peter)

You are at lesson 25. If you are doing these according to schedule, you are just one month away from completing this curriculum. Can you believe how fast a year goes by? You are a year older and I know that if you are doing these lessons as they are to be done, you have gained much knowledge and wisdom. I am blessed to be part of this journey that you are on. Okay, lesson 25 will be about two of the three apostles that were with Jesus more than any of the other apostles. Just like the apostle Paul, these two apostles bring truth that encourages, warns, guides and applies. All these things will make sense as you live out your faith. You may be thinking that the Bible sure seems to talk a lot about suffering. You may have thought that this "Christian" thing was about being happy and getting stuff. Actually, your salvation is about God and living in obedience so that you will understand true joy, not happiness. Happiness is defined as circumstantial, but joy is an "all the time thing." When things do not go your way, does your mood always change? If so, then you are experiencing happiness, not joy. The joy of Christ will change you so that even what the world calls unlucky or complains about, you will see the ultimate joy in it. If you are not there yet, that is okay. Remember this is a journey.

<u>JAMES</u>

James, the brother of Jesus, focuses on faith and suffering within an obedient life in God, and what this should look like in your life. He is bold in saying what is true and what is false. Are you ready to see more consistency of Scripture?

1. James, the brother of Jesus, wastes no time in telling you that you should expect to have

_____. Testing of your _____ produces steadfastness so that you may be

perfect and _____(also see verse 12). In verse 5, he goes on to say that if you lack

_____, you should _____ God for it.

- Have you realized that your salvation is a journey for the rest of your life, and thus you need to be equipped on this "Journey". What did you just read about being equipped?

- **Illustration**: You are the running back on your high school football team and you are about to run your first play, but you only have your basketball shoes, uniform and your shoulder pads. You have no helmet or any other pads. Are you equipped or are you about to get hurt?

- In 1:13-16, James tells us God cannot be tempted, but you can. So be equipped against temptations of Satan and against temptations that dwell in you, as a sinful man/woman.

- Can you deceive yourself and what are the cures for this problem? 1:19-25

201

- How does James summarize about what you should be doing in 1:27? What is he trying to say?

2. Read James 2:1-13 and write down the main sin that is happening here.

> I have to say that in our schools, this sin is often more harmful than any other. Can you be honest with yourself and list examples of where you struggle with this. Can you also think of how you may see it? Do you help those who always seem to be left out or may be a little different?

3. Read 2:14-26 about faith. James teaches the truth that faith will contain works, and faith will have action. You have been learning this consistent truth since Genesis.

- "So also faith by itself, if it does not have works, is _____."
- He goes on to compare faith with works and faith without works. I will show you my _____ by my works.
- "You believe that God is one; you do well. Even the _____ believe and shudder. In other words, to say you have faith, but do no works puts you in the same category as the _____(not where you want to be).
- What examples does James give to solidify his point?

4. Read James 3:1-12 and 5:13-20 in closing.

> How many of you are teachers? Actually all believers are teachers in one sense or another. After all, you have salvation, you have hope and there is a world full of people that need to hear this. But when you speak, make sure your tongue speaks truth. The tongue is a powerful thing and influences for good and for evil. Use your testimony and the basic truths you are learning in this curriculum to speak truth to others.

> **Critical Thought: The Tongue**: List an area in your life where your tongue seems to get you in trouble. Yes I am assuming you have one area because almost everyone does, including me.

- What does confession of sins bring in your life?

1 PETER

5. Peter, the one who denied Jesus the Christ 3 times, goes on to be a powerful witness for the gospel.

- What kind of inheritance awaits those who are saved and who guards it? After you find out who guards it, does that make you feel good?
.
- In 1 Peter 1:14-16, Peter says that before you were saved, you were _____ and do not be _____ by these passions. Look back at Romans 12:1-2.

- Peter then quotes Leviticus 19:2 and it says what?

6. In 2:22, Peter refers to Jesus the Christ as our example of suffering. People will say bad things about you just as they Jesus, but He did not return evil for evil. 1 Peter 3:9, Proverbs 3:7, 8:13.

- **Yeshua was without sin and thus our perfect sacrifice, the only one (God's Son came in flesh), who could ever take away our sins and restore our honor. Sinful man cannot save sinful man.**

- In 3:14 and 4:12, Peter continues to talk about suffering for good. After all, suffering for what is evil will not be rewarded.

  - ➤ Have you suffered for doing what is right this past year? If not, you have to ask yourself why there is no suffering. Are you a stealth Christian, hiding where no one knows? Are you afraid to stand up for injustice that you see in your school or work?

7. 2 Peter begins by talking about how important it is to have the knowledge of God.

- In verse 8, Peter says, "If these qualities are yours and _____, they keep you from being ineffective or _____ in the knowledge of our Lord Jesus Christ."

- What qualities is Peter referring to in verses 5-8?

- Are you saved to bear fruit or be unfruitful?

- Why is it important to increase and not just stay the same? See Hebrews 5:12-14, I Peter 2:2. **Remember God has saved you to change you.**

- If you do not grow in these qualities, you will be _____, nearsighted and

   _____ that your sins are cleansed by the sinless blood of Jesus the Christ. 1:9

8. Extreme Thought: The Word of God- Peter makes one of the most powerful statements in the entire Bible in 1:16-21. Peter, James and John saw and experienced God's presence and proclamation that Yeshua was His Son in Matthew 17:1-8. Now Peter says here that the **prophetic word, the Bible** that you now hold in your hand, is "even more sure" than his eyewitness experience. Also see Yeshua's response in Luke 16:31. He does not say that it is Him that they need to know in order to be saved, but that it is Moses, who represented the Law of God, and the Prophets. He said this because walking in the Law of Moses, thus walking in the Word and Yeshua is the walking Word of God. It is all connected.

Do you think knowing His Word is of any significance? Think about it. Yeshua did nothing outside of walking in the Laws of God and fulfilling prophecy. So when you follow the commands of God, you are emulating God the Father and His Son, whom He sent to reveal the Father. He could do no other. May we also walk in obedience! (Refer back to Lesson 19 #14 and John 5:39).

Do you know how privileged you are to live in a country where Bibles, curriculum, sermons on the Internet, radio, etc. are so accessible? You can study God's Word anytime you want. There are people in other countries that would and do literally die attempting to acquire and read their Bibles. Many of them have to read them by dim light at night so no one will take them to prison or kill them. Take a moment and pray for these men and women as instructed in Hebrews 13:3. Also, hold your Bible as precious as your very next breath. It is you know!

9. Peter warns of false prophets and false teachers.

- Who else warns about them in Matthew 24:11, 24, Luke 6:26?

- If they warn against false teachers and false prophets, then you need to be aware that there are those that will deceive. Also see book of Jude (only 1 chapter so read it now and write a few thoughts).

- What will equip you to fight this and know truth? What did you just read in chapter 1?

10. In 2 Peter 3:1-7, he continues to warn against false teachers, calling them scoffers.

- In verses 4-6, he refers to what event that took place in Genesis involving a lot of water?

- Did the flood change anything? Refer to Lesson 4 #1. Again, you can also go to *www.answersingenesis.org*. Hopefully, you have already been to the website.

- In 3:13, you are to wait for a new _____ and _____ earth (Revelation 3:12, 21:1-5).

- Who will dwell in the new earth? Also read Matthew 13:39-43.

- What happens to the unrighteous? Matthew 13:39-43, 24:36-39, Luke 17:32-37

11. Peter ends by giving a final warning about false teachers and teachings. In 3:15, he even says that Paul's writings are tough to understand but that we should pay attention to what he has to say. You can trust Paul's writings because Paul obeyed the laws of God. Many different interpretations and opinions are out there about God and His Word. Pray and study so that you will show yourself approved by God. 2 Timothy 2:15. Do not be discouraged. You are learning each time you open the Word of God.

A. Memory Verse: James 1:19 and 1:22 (Write them out here).

B. Six questions to ask while thinking back through the text.

1. Who is sure of their salvation? 2Peter1

2. What does James say is absolutely important to prove your faith?

3. When did God's creation change?

4. Where will you dwell if you are here when Jesus returns?

5. Why are your works important each day?

6. How do you know you are a believer?

C. Application How does this biblical truth affect how I live my life each day? Does this explain what you see in the news each day or what you see in your family and friends?

D. Journal and prayer time. Is there a sin you need to confess? As you do this, ask God to help you live according to what you have just studied. Praise God for wisdom in discerning between what is true and what is false.

Lesson 26: You Will Win, Live Like Winners- (I John and Revelation)

You may be thinking, "Yes I am finally finished." Yes you are finishing this curriculum, but remember in the introduction that the goal is not just to finish the curriculum, but also to be changed by studying the Word of God. I pray that you are not the same person you were a year ago. I pray that this is just the beginning to many more years of finishing curriculums, personal studies, digging deeper to find more levels of Scripture that God wants to teach you, etc. My follow up "The Journey Part 2" should be ready by the time you finish this. Keep growing and never stop being a disciple of Yeshua the Messiah. Remember that Yeshua means salvation, so when you are in Him you are to display salvation to those around you (Galatians 2:20). You will never do it perfectly, but are you striving, walking towards Him daily? Torah is defined as pointing to the direction you should walk and righteousness is defined as a straight path, so follow the commands of God along His straight path and you will see His blessings. Maybe the blessings will not look like you think they should in that moment, but you will look back like I have over my life and see His faithfulness to meet my needs in every area of my life. He will do the same for you. Are you ready for this last lesson? I know I am. Let's go!

1. John, the other apostle of the three closest apostles (James and Peter) to Yeshua, writes 3 letters called 1, 2 and 3rd John and Revelation. We will just spend time in 1 John and Revelation.

2. First John is a book that teaches you that if you do not love your fellow believers then you do not love God (2:9, 3:15, 4:20). That sounds pretty harsh, but it emphasizes what you have already studied from Romans 12 and other places concerning how believers treat other believers. It also emphasizes the holiness of God and your purpose for living is to glorify Him.

- In 1:6-7 says, "If we say we have _____ with _____ while we walk in _____, we lie and do not practice the truth. But if we walk in the _____ as he is in the _____, we have fellowship with one _____ and the blood of Jesus his Son cleanses us from all sin."

- This verse shows you that light and darkness do not mix (2 Corinthians 6:14). It also shows you that when you walk in the light it restores your relationship with one another and thus with God. **You cannot separate how you love your fellow believer from how you love God. One reflects the other**.

3. In 1:9, John says "If we _____ our sins, He is _____ and _____ to forgive us and to cleanse us from all unrighteousness."

- Is God always faithful and just?
- Is it dependent upon us if he is faithful and just? So how do we get to experience this?

4. 1n 2:15-17, you see a contrast between the worldview of those that are lost and those that are of God. List some differences here.

5. In 4:1-4, John talks about testing the false spirits in the world. Peter also warned about the same false prophets and to know truth.

- John tells them in 4:4 that they have overcome these false spirits and how do you know this? What is the context of what these believers are experiencing?

6. What are the opposites of love and why? Did you think it was just one thing as I did (John 14:15, 21, I John 3:11-15, 4:17-18)? What does abide mean in 3:14 (google abide definition Hebrew)?

> **Definitive Thought: Love and Fear**: I have decided to focus on fear for now. If you are like me, you thought only love and hate were opposites. To walk in fear is to walk in a state that keeps you from receiving God's best. This is why the idea of fear and love is stated in the context of loving one another. To love one another reveals God's love for you. To walk in fear is to block out or lessen the understanding and experience of God's amazing love for you. To live in fear paralyzes, restricts and removes the full benefits that we can receive each day from our God. To fear anything other than God, shows us that we are not walking in faith or trusting God. To walk in fear is to claim, even if you do not mean to do so, you are trusting more in yourself than in God. God loves you so much and wants you to live out your best for Him. Don't let fear cause you to miss out on so many blessings that God has for you, to ultimately miss out on His love and the love you can have for others.

> **Illustration:** If someone says, I choose to live in homosexuality and it is okay because God loves me. This is someone that unfortunately does not understand love or the opposites of love. This is commonly seen today in the battle to make homosexuality a norm in our culture or for people to believe that they can be Christians and yet embrace homosexuality or any other sin. Notice I said embrace, not to sin unintentional or to struggle with sin but wanting to live for God. There is a difference. When you see love in Scripture, the first understanding is loyalty or commitment. So in response we are to love like God first loved us (Read 1 John 4:19, Romans 5:6-8), and thus we will walk in a committed life to His way, not ours. Morality is objective, not subjective. Does God love us on our terms or His terms? Is it His morality or ours?

7. In 3:4-9 and 5:18, John clearly states that a believer will not keep on _____.
Now he is not saying that you have the ability to be sinless, but your daily practice should not reflect sinfulness. Therefore, if you constantly sin, you are not living like Christ is in you, but you are living just the opposite, thus bearing no fruit for God.

> **Extreme Thought: Repentance**- If you know you will sin, but you are not supposed to sin, what can you do about this? When you sin, you need to own up to it. Repenting according to 2 Corinthians 7 and Numbers 5 will set you apart in this world. People will be shocked when you come back and ask for forgiveness and make it right, whether it be returning something you borrowed a long time ago or maybe you stole or telling them that you were wrong when you got angry or gossiped about them. You will be amazed how much respect this will earn you and you can now easily talk about the love of Christ and share the full gospel with them. Pray about this today and everyday.

REVELATION

8. The last book of the Bible—Revelation Of Yeshua, the Anointed One.

- Before I begin this summary, I will just tell you that this is a book that has been interpreted by many people and in many different ways. I am not attempting to, nor do I even have time, to get into many of the details. I will just touch on a few highlights as I have with many other books up to this point.

> John is writing this while in exile on an island. Has anyone ever heard of Alcatraz, which is an island near New York City? I actually went there, not as a prisoner, but as a tourist a few years ago. John is a prisoner and God reveals many things to him and he writes them down. You are now reading what he has written.

9. "I Am the _____ and the _____, says the Lord God, who is and who was and who is to come, the Almighty." What do these Greek words mean? See Exodus 3:14

- Who lives forevermore and is before all and died?

10. In chapters 2 and 3, he writes to 7 churches and he looks at their works to see if they have honored their God. He tells them what they have done wrong and right and reminds them what will happen if they do not repent.

11. God created everything with a purpose including the angels. Compare this with Isaiah 6:1-6, which is where John is quoting from. Revelation 4:8.

- In 4:11, John writes, "_____ are you, our Lord and God, to receive glory and honor and power, for you created _____ things and by your _____ they existed and were created."

- In 7:13, there are the righteous (wearing white robes) who have made it through the tribulation period. "They have washed their robes in the blood of the _____." Read Exodus 19:14, Revelation 19:8 concerning the washing of garments (robes of righteousness before a holy God).

- As you studied in lesson 25 #10, the righteous will inhabit the earth, so if God wills that they go through the tribulation, then He is able to protect them during this time or allow them to die, both of which reflect the reality of life and of our faithful God.

> ➤ It seems ironic to us to think that something would be made clean by blood, but instead we think that blood is unclean. However, blood flows through your body and keeps you alive physically and the blood that Jesus shed for you makes you clean spiritually. If you are saved, you entered into a blood covenant (Lesson 8 #10). Are you living like you have been washed by the blood of a sinless Savior?

12. In Revelation 11:15, God will restore the earth and His kingdom will be here on earth as it is in heaven (Matthew 6:10). Also read 11:19 and refer back to Exodus 19:18 and 25:9.

13. In 12:7-17, the dragon or _____ makes war on the rest of the woman's _____ (seed). Remember Genesis 3:15 and Galatians 3:16. There is a seed of the woman and all that come from her are offspring of righteousness or those that _____ the commandments of God. And the seed of the serpent, or Satan, are the offspring of unrighteousness.

> ➤ Do you realize how consistent the Scriptures of God are? I have continually sent you back and forth in various books of the Bible so that you can see the consistency of the God over all things, the God of salvation. This is the last book of the Bible and we can still refer back to Genesis, the first book of the Bible. God is truth.

14. In Revelation 15:5, John writes, "After this I looked and the sanctuary (Holy of Holies) of the tent of witness in _____ was opened." This is the Holy of Holies in the heavenly temple. Moses saw the pattern in heaven and built it on earth. Exodus 25:9, Matthew 6:10. The temple may have been destroyed on earth, but the heavenly temple still exists, but it will not come down until Yeshua comes back (Revelation 21:1-2).

15. In 17:14, John writes "They will make war on the Lamb, and the Lamb will conquer them, for he is _____ of lords and _____ of kings, and those with him are called and chosen and faithful." Also see 19:16.

- If you are a believer, you win the battle, the war, etc. You are on the winning team, the Y'shua team, the team of hope, victory and salvation. Rejoice in this great truth.

16. In Revelation 19:6-14, the saints have clothed themselves in white robes (righteousness) in anticipation of the _____ supper of the Lamb. He has come to take care of His _____.

17. In 19:13, Yeshua comes clothed in a robe dipped in blood and He is called the Word of God. See Lesson 23 #1.

18. In Revelation chapter 20, an _____ comes down and throws _____ into the bottomless pit for 1,000 years.

- What happens after the 1,000 years? 20:7-10

- A great judgment takes place next and anyone's name not found in the Lamb's _____ of life, is thrown into the lake of _____.

19. In 21:1-4, what will be no more? List the 6 things

20. In 21:9-27, John describes the holy city of Jerusalem in all of its beauty.

- What will be no more? 22-26

- How will there be light? How awesome is this!

> **Critical Thought: Are You Saved?** John again mentions the Lamb's book of _____ like he does in 20:15. Look at Deuteronomy 32:32-33 and you see that your name can be written in the Book of Life and it can be blotted out. Are you secure in salvation in the hands of God? Yes you are if you want to stay in, but just like on an earthly kingdom, you can choose to walk out in rebellion, you can do the same in the Heavenly Kingdom. Have you been doing this curriculum because you think someone expects this of you or are you saved and you truly desire to serve God and be a disciple of Jesus the Christ? No one can tell you if you are saved or not, because this is between you and God. How are you living? Is your desire to truly please God by walking in His ways? If you are not sure if your name is written in the Book of Life, you need to make sure. You only have one life and one judgment. Hebrews 9:27. See Lesson 5 #7 about faith and salvation.

21. In reading Revelation 22:1-5, it will benefit you to go back to Genesis chapters 2-3.

- How many trees are their now and which one is left?
- No longer will there be anything _____ as it has been for about 6000 years (Genesis 3).

22. Revelation 22:10-21.

- In verse 11, there is mention of something that you have read many times in this curriculum and that is the fact that there are only two kinds of people—_____ and _____. Until the very end, they will exist together. Therefore be concerned and zealous for what is right, but do not be surprised by the sinfulness of man and how bad things can get at times.

- Who has the right to the tree of life?

- How does Jesus describe Himself in 22:16? Isaiah 11:10, 53:2, 2 Samuel 7:16, Matthew 1:1, John 7:42, 2 Peter 1:19, Revelation 2:28.

- The last warning is about adding or taking away from the Word, which is adding or taking away from God, the Savior, the Lord, the King over all. The Scriptures are to be proclaimed as truth and are sufficient on their own. (Deuteronomy 4:2, 12:32, Proverbs 30:5-6). It is okay to study and attempt to figure out things and it is okay to have opinions about things that you are not clear about. However, do not say that the word says something when it does not. God is serious about His word since He wrote it and has revealed it to those that have washed their robes (their lives) in righteousness.

A. Memory Verse: 1 John 1:9-10, Revelation 21:6 (Write them out).

B. Six questions to ask while thinking back through the text.

1. Who wins the battle forever?

2. What will happen to Satan?

3. When can you add or take away words from the revelation of God?

4. Where will believers spend eternity?

5. Why do people go to Hell and does God send them there? Revelation 21

6. How do we have light in the end?

C. Application How does this biblical truth affect how I live my life each day?

D. Journal and prayer time. Is there a sin you need to confess? Praise God for His salvation and victory within you through Yeshua!

CLOSING COMMENTS

I wanted to take a moment to congratulate you students on this huge accomplishment. I do not know if you realize how few Christians ever go through this much discipleship material or ever go through the Bible chronologically which means you have learned about God by setting the correct foundation according to His order. This is something to be proud of and more important, it is something that you need to continually refer to as you grow with the Lord. After all, the material you have learned is the foundation of your journey. Everything you do after this should build upon this study.

I have prayed for those that are going through this curriculum and I would love to hear from you after you finish. Go to **www.only1way.net** and keep in touch if you can. It is always great to hear from those that are doing this curriculum, as well as those that have completed it. I should have the second year study done by now, if God wills it. Thank you for allowing me to walk with you on this year of your journey. May it be the first of many and may your daily decisions be ones that focus upon the Tree of Life; Genesis 2:9, 16-17, Revelation 22:14.

In Y'shua

Paul Sommer

BIBLIOGRAPHY

Benner, Jeff, The Ancient Hebrew Lexicon of the Bible. College Station, TX: Virtualbookworm.com Publishing, Inc. 2005.

Booker, Richard, The Miracle of the Scarlet Thread. Shippensburg, PA: Destiny Image Publishers, Inc. 2008.

Hatch, Edwin and Redpath, Henry A., A Concordance to the Septuagint: And the Other Greek Versions of the Old Testament (Including the Apocryphal Books). Grand Rapids, MI: Baker Books, 1998.

Scott, Bradford, The Tanakh: The Dictionary of the New Testament. Littleton, CO: Children Are Forever Publishing, 2009.

Strong, James, Strong's Exhaustive Concordance, 1890. Electronic Edition from Rick Meyers, e-Sword Version 7.8.5: Franklin, TN: 2007.

James Swanson, Dictionary of Biblical Languages with Semantic Domains: Hebrew (Old Testament), electronic edition Oak Harbor: Logos Research Systems, Inc.

Glossary of Terms

1. **Atonement**- Lesson 10, Pg. 77

2. **Blessing**- Lesson 6, Pg. 49.

3. **Covenant-** Lesson 8, Pg. 62.

4. **Faith (belief) defined**- Lesson 5, Pg. 41.

5. **Gospel defined**- Lesson 5, Pg. 39.

6. **Grace**- Lesson 2, Pg. 24.

7. **Holiness (of God) defined**- Lesson 10, Pg. 76.

8. **Holiness (of man) defined**- Lesson 10, Pg. 78.

9. **Holy Spirit defined**- Lesson 19, Pg. 150.

10. **Image defined**- Lesson 4, Pg. 36.

11. **Justified Defined**- Lesson 24, Pg. 193.

12. **Offering Defined**- Lesson 3, Pg. 29.

13. **Prayer defined**- Lesson 19, Pg. 154.

14. **Redeem-** Lesson 8, Pg. 60.

15. **Repentance defined**- Lesson 10, Pg. 77.

16. **Righteousness defined**- Lesson 7, Pg. 54.

17. **Salvation defined**-Lesson 5, Pg. 41.

18. **Sin Defined**- Lesson 2, Pg. 22.

19. **Statute Defined**- Lesson 16, Pg. 126.

20. **Torah (Law) Defined**- Lesson 15, Pg. 116.

21. **Truth defined**- Lesson 20, Pg. 164.

22. **Wise (wisdom) defined**- Lesson 15, Pg. 114.

23. **Worship defined**- Lesson 5, Pg. 40

Endnotes

1. Strong, James. Strong's Exhaustive Concordance 1890, Electronic Edition (H2398 and H2403), and Benner, Jeff A. The Ancient Hebrew Lexicon of the Bible, 2005, (Sin) 121.

2. Strong, James (H2580 and H2603) and Benner, Jeff A., (Grace/Favor), 126.

3. Strong, James (H4503) and Benner, Jeff A., (Offering), 182.

4. Strong, James (H6754) and Benner, Jeff A., (Image), 425.

5. Hatch, Edwin and Redpath, Henry A., A Concordance to the Septuagint: And the Other Greek Versions of the Old Testament (Including the Apocryphal Books). Grand Rapids, MI: Baker Books, 1998, 586. Strong, James (G4283, G2098, H1319) and Benner, Jeff A., (Gospel), 306.

6. Strong, James (H7812) and Benner, Jeff A., (Worship), 275.

7. Strong, James (H539, H540); Benner, Jeff A., (Faith)170-171.

8. Strong, James (H3444, H3467) and Benner, Jeff A., (Salvation), 281-282.

9. Strong, James (H1288) and Benner, Jeff A., (Bless or Blessing), 309.

10. Strong, James (H6666 and H6662) and Benner, Jeff A., (Righteousness), 424.

11. Strong, James (H1350) and Benner, Jeff A., (Redeem), 82.

12. Swanson, James, Dictionary of Biblical Languages with Semantic Domains: Hebrew (Old Testament), electronic edition Oak Harbor: Logos Research Systems, Inc., (Name), (9005 from Strong's H8034).

13. Booker, Richard, The Miracle of the Scarlet Thread. Shippensburg, PA: Destiny Image Publishers, Inc. 2008, (Covenant), 34-41.

14. Scott, Bradford, The Tanakh: The Dictionary of the New Testament. Children Are Forever Publishing, 2009, (Y'shua) 93.

15. Strong, James (H3722) and Benner, Jeff A., (Atonement), 356-357.

16. Strong, James (H5162 and H7725) and Benner, Jeff A., (Repentance), 272, 377.

17. Strong, James (H6944 or 6918) and Benner, Jeff., (Holiness of man), 433.

18. Swanson, James (4595 from Strong H4150 and H3259); (Moedim).

19. Strong, James (H6035) and Benner, Jeff A. (Meek), 212.

20. Strong, James (H2451 and H7919) and Benner, Jeff A., (Wise or Wisdom) 391.

21. Strong, James (H8451) and Benner, Jeff A., (Torah) 142-143.

22. Strong, James (H2706, H2708) and Benner, Jeff A., (Statute) 129-130.

23. Strong, James (H6419) and Benner, Jeff A., (Prayer) 221.

24. Strong, James (H571 and H3651) and Benner, Jeff A., (Truth) Pages 171 and 149.

25. Strong, James (G1344 and H6663) and Benner, Jeff A., (Justified) 424.